STUDIES IN INTELLECTUAL BREAKTHROUGH

CHARLES DAVID AXELROD

STUDIES IN INTELLECTUAL

BREAKTHROUGH

FREUD
SIMMEL
BUBER

University of Massachusetts Press   Amherst

Library of Congress Catalog Card Number 78–53177
ISBN 0–87023–256–8
Printed in the United States of America
Designed by Mary Mendell
Library of Congress Cataloging in Publication Data
appear on the last page of the book

Grateful acknowledgment is made to the following for permission to reprint copyrighted material:

Basic Books, for quotations from "Further Recommendations in the Technique of Psycho-Analysis," in *The Collected Papers of Sigmund Freud*, volume 2, edited by Ernest Jones, M.D. Authorized translation under the supervision of Joan Riviere. Published by Basic Books, Inc., Publishers, New York, by arrangement with The Hogarth Press Ltd. and The Institute of Psycho-Analysis, London.

Elsevier Scientific Publishing Company, for "Freud and Science," in *Theory and Society* 4 (1977), pp. 273–94. Reprinted with permission of Elsevier Scientific Publishing Company, Amsterdam.

Hogarth Press for quotations from volume 12 of the *Standard Edition of the Complete Psychological Works of Sigmund Freud*, translated and edited by James Strachey. London: Hogarth Press.

The Sociological Quarterly, for "Toward an Appreciation of Simmel's Fragmentary Style." Copyright © 1977 by the Midwest Sociological Society.

The Macmillan Company, for quotations from Kurt H. Wolff, *The Sociology of Georg Simmel*. Copyright © 1950 by The Free Press.

To my friend and teacher
JOHANN W. MOHR

ACKNOWLEDGMENTS

I am grateful to the Canada Council and to the Ministry of Colleges and Universities of the Province of Ontario for funding me during the writing of this book; and to the Canada Council Funds Committee of the University of Manitoba for helping with the costs of its final preparation.

The following colleagues have criticized all or parts of the manuscript, or helped in the formulation of its central themes: Johann W. Mohr, Kenneth Morrison, Raymond Morrow, Mark W. Novak, Gottfried Paasche, James Porter, Nicholas Tavuchis, and Kurt H. Wolff.

I want to express my gratitude to Richard Martin, Carol Schoen and the rest of the staff at the University of Massachusetts Press for their congeniality and excellent editorial advice.

Finally, I thank my wife Sara, and my children Tami Amanda and Deborah Shaine—no particulars can sum up these relationships.

CONTENTS

1
INTELLECTUAL BREAKTHROUGH AND ITS CONCEPTUAL FIELD

I   We are accustomed to conceiving of intellectual breakthrough solely in terms of some completed achievement—a new law, a new style, a new paradigm. We can recall clearly, neatly, concisely, Newton's laws of motion, Darwin's theory of evolution, Freud's theories of neurosis and infantile sexuality. We seldom, however, conceive of intellectual breakthrough as a social phenomenon, as a discourse through which the "product" materialized within the social world.

Yet what are we left with when we can recall the articulated product but not its formative process, when we can no longer see the relation between the result of an inquiry and its coming into being? Hegel claims that we are left with a corpse. "The result," he says, "[is not] the actual whole, but only the result together with its becoming." [1] To recall a product of intellectual breakthrough while forgetting the analytic conditions of its utterance is to have the answer but no memory of the question.[2] To report a discourse by segregating it from its process is to constrict its nature and diminish its potential. If intellectual achievements interest us at all, we should wish to account for the answers they give in terms of their aims, commitments, struggles, necessity—in short, their "forms of life." [3]

How, then, can we conceive of this relation between the completed achievement and its processes of coming into being? Is the discursive event so independent of its product that we must bring the two together synthetically? Hardly. To conceive of them as separate is to have manufactured that separation. Although the formative process may elude us once the inquiry is over, its product continually intimates its existence. Our task, then, is to penetrate the product and uncover what resides in its tacit dimensions.[4]

These essays investigate empirically the topic of intellectual breakthrough by examining the works of Sigmund Freud, Georg Simmel, and Martin Buber. The essays have a dual purpose: first, to place (replace) each of these authors within the discursive event in which he was involved, and second, to treat the author's work as an occasion to address the wider topic of intellectual breakthrough. Although Freud, Simmel, and Buber are certainly interesting in and by themselves, this study addresses, in particular, their ability to make transparent certain questions at the heart of the concept of "breakthrough": questions about thinking, individuality, and community.

A large body of literature relating to intellectual breakthrough has already appeared. In general it attempts to account for those individuals who set a new course of inquiry, who create an original idea or work, whose thinking is out of the ordinary yet compelling to a wide audience. This literature has at various times used the terms "creativity," "intellectual revolution," "iconoclasm," "genius," "breakthrough," "invention," terms which at first seem to reflect different orientations to the phenomenon. But it would be more accurate to say that *each term does its part to create the phenomenon it then proceeds to describe.* Thus the grammar of the term "creativity" does not point to exactly the same events as the grammar of "iconoclasm." Similarly, the "genius" is not quite the same person analytically as the "prodigy," nor is "intellectual breakthrough" necessarily the same process as "intellectual revolution." Each term opens its own phenomenal field and at the same time dictates its boundaries. I have chosen the term "intellectual breakthrough" in order to accent social processes; this term refers not only to the finished product of inquiry (as later summarized in textbooks and history books) but, in its notion of "breaking through," also speaks to an accompanying discursive tension.

Tension, as we commonly use the term, refers to a strain placed on an object. Discursive tension, then, refers to a strain that an inquiry places on an idea or conceptual field. However, since inquiry and discourse manifest themselves in relations between people, they determine and also assume the character of those relations. Ideas do not float freely among people; they become rooted in commitments, ossified and sustained within intellectual communities; they are cradled among avid sponsors and defenders whose work relies on their stability. Thus the tension of discourse refers not merely to the presence of one language addressing (and straining) another, but to the presence of one language addressing the inertia of another. We can almost picture the individual inquirer pulling on the locked gates of a conceptual castle—pulling on them from the inside.

The idea of intellectual breakthrough derives its unique signature from this discursive tension that it subsumes. The term treats inquiry and intellectual achievement sociologically by placing them in relation to socially situated (delimited) ideas and conceptual fields. As such, the idea of breakthrough refers to an essential feature of intellectual relations, and of human relations in general: the tension between the individual and the group. The term intellectual breakthrough points precisely to this particular tension. Other words which are often considered synonymous and used interchangeably carry quite different connotations. "Creativity" and "invention," for example, do not signify tension or struggle at all, although struggle may often accompany them. The word "revolution" also ignores this particular theme; revolution, of course, does imply tension, but the tension immanent to this term is not between an individual and a group, but between one group and another.

My purpose, then, is to enunciate an essential dynamic of social life that has too often been forgotten; to the extent that the tension between the individual and the group is persistently defeated, silenced, made to appear irrelevant to everyday social life, the task of bringing it to the surface presents an important challenge to any inquiry. Freud, Simmel, and Buber will aid in this challenge.

II

To address intellectual breakthrough or related phenomena, it may first be appropriate to consult those constructs that others have already developed. However, a word of caution: though a pregiven construct might make it easy for us to start, it could make it difficult for us to proceed effectively if the construct we choose inadvertently debars us from what is central to the topic. Beginnings are too crucial and decisive for us to rely merrily on the authority of convention. Therefore a careful beginning is advisable; we *should* consult available constructs to benefit from previous inquiry, but we should first try to determine their adequacy as formulations of the topic.

The Stranger   For the sociological community, the construct "stranger" contains certain directions for the study of intellectual breakthrough as a particular instance of the tension between the individual and the group. First formulated in Georg Simmel's essay, "The Stranger," [5] and then reformulated by Robert Ezra Park,[6] Everett Stonequist,[7] and Alfred Schutz,[8] to name a few, the stranger has become an often-used metaphor for various themes of social relations, and has occasionally been used to explain the capacity for and processes of intellectual achievement. The stranger—the person attached to the group from the outside—is both near the group (in the sense that he participates in group life), and distant (in the sense that he has not participated in it from the beginning, and "imports qualities into it which do not and cannot stem from the group itself" [9]). This unity of nearness and distance maps out the formal position of the stranger.

While the stranger constitutes a special category of membership, he is only formulable *in contrast to* the full-fledged members. In other words, the stranger only becomes visible—and then sociologically significant—as a construct of difference. We define him with reference to differences; discussions about him generate formulations of that from which he differs. Most important, however, the stranger illuminates categories of difference regarding measures and meanings of membership.

Unlike other sociological constructs of the individual (such as Parson's "collectivity member" and Goffman's "role player") where the individual is formulated simply as a part of a well-run machine which runs so smoothly that it successfully obscures the particularity of its parts, the stranger is never so integrated into the group as to become imperceptible. But neither is he so distant as to become irrelevant to social relations. Hence the stranger as a construct built on difference preserves the category "individual," but does so *as a viable sociological category* which can be made to represent generally the tension between the individual and the group.

If we formulate the stranger in ostensibly negative terms (e.g., socially unbalanced, awkward, unknowledgeable about the niceties of custom), then his conceptual negation—the full-fledged member— can be considered correspondingly in positive terms (e.g., stable, refined, knowledgeable). However, we can also formulate the stranger inversely, noting his formal potential for being less controlled by the pregivens of a particular culture. Coming from the outside, and therefore open to a wider world than is the full-fledged member, the stranger can more easily remain unshackled by "sacred" tradition. Simmel discusses the stranger as one who has a heightened potential for rendering impartial judgments.[10] Veblen notes the disproportionately high number of strangers among pathfinders and iconoclasts.[11] Behind these perceptions, of course, lies an understanding of the "other side" of membership: its narrowing and confining capacity. Viewed in this light, the stranger generates a version of membership as the abandonment of authentic reflection, as blind obedience to institutions, and as the repression and defeat of doubt.

To the extent that the stranger does reveal this repressive side of membership, he also invokes a particular conception of inquiry. In this context inquiry does not simply involve the linear build-up or accumulation of knowledge, that is, the addition of new knowledge to the old; for to accumulate knowledge linearly presumes fixed and unquestioned methods of accumulation, fixed directions of investigation, and underlying these, fixed grounds. Inquiry of the sort invoked by the stranger involves the capacity to question, even to violate, what has already been accumulated and accepted within the community. More precisely, inquiry in this sense addresses (readdresses) the grounds upon which the accumulation took place. Thus membership and strangership differ in relation to inquiry by virtue of their differing relation to grounds. The stranger, as a construct that distinguishes the individual from the group, also distinguishes a vantage position from which inquiry (as dis-course) takes place; and the unity of nearness and distance embodied in the stranger symbolizes the analytic (the necessary) conditions of such inquiry.

Nevertheless the construct has certain clearly defined limits. While the stranger can turn his social relations into a seedbed of discourse, he can also turn them into a condition of heightened conformity. (Don't converts often make the most aggressively disciplined followers?)[12] Thus while one perception of the stranger generates a metaphor for enunciated individuality, a second inversely creates a metaphor for compulsive obedience.

This unity of opposites on the level of metaphor renders the construct unusable as an explanation of any particular intellectual breakthrough. To account for breakthrough by referring only to its author's estrangement neglects the fact that estrangement works in several ways.[13] Reference to an author's estrangement does not by itself bridge the gap between the potential for achievement and its actualization, because not everyone with potential makes use of it. The fact of estrangement does not guarantee a product, and the formula "step outside and be creative" is a prescription for nothing in particular. It would be even more misleading to explain a particular breakthrough by mentioning that its author came from outside the community—as "Einstein was a Jew." Such explanations, of which there are many, confuse metaphor and homologue by wrongly treating estrangement as a structural feature of citizenship, ethnic background, religion, or place of origin.

Hence "the stranger" has its limits, but these limits can still encompass a fertile construct. In the sense that estrangement can be understood as a necessary ingredient of discourse, and in the sense that intellectual relations are pervasively also social relations, then on the level of generality the sociological construct of "the stranger" provides a useful metaphor that can suggest implications for inquiry and, for our purposes, intellectual breakthrough.

Thomas Kuhn and the Structure of Scientific Revolutions   The categories of inquiry metaphorically represented in the stranger have been discussed concretely by a number of contemporary historians and philosophers of science, one of the more prominent of whom is Thomas Kuhn. In *The Structure of Scientific Revolutions*,[14] Kuhn analyzes paradigm shifts within the scientific community and the works of the individuals who initiated them. Although Kuhn organizes his discussion in the context of the natural sciences alone, certain more salient features of his analysis go beyond the domain of natural science and refer to the processes that accompany the institutionalization of all intellectual activity.[15]

Kuhn begins his discussion by addressing a particular misconception that science has of itself: that science is necessarily a cumulative enterprise. According to this view, the scientific community is a monistic one whose theoretical foundation and all previous scientific achievements are viewed as steppingstones for any work that follows. The history of science is thus conceived of as the uninterrupted linear progression toward the truth. Each scientist's completed work becomes reified, communally owned, and available to all members as a resource for their work.[16]

Kuhn argues, however, that it is in the interest of the enterprise to believe that science is cumulative regardless of whether or not it is, for such a belief (faith) functions to stabilize the achieved theoretical foundation of the scientific community. According to Kuhn, science requires that its members rely on secured foundations in order for normal scientific work to proceed, for without a secure framework, members would tend to continually reexamine their first principles. This would only delay the "business" of science, which is the accumulation of knowledge through problem-solving. To the extent that this really is the business of science (a judgment which is in itself worthy of reconsideration), then the notion of science as cumulative is not merely a description of the character of science but a positive value upheld within the community. As Kuhn notes, this ideology plays an important pedagogical role in the education of scientists. During the course of his training, the would-be scientist is given a theoretical foundation on which to build, and learns to regard the foundation as a secured and trustworthy accomplishment achieved once and for all.[17]

When this cumulative nature of the enterprise is stressed in the training of scientists, it generally becomes a self-fulfilling prophesy. According to Kuhn, members normally accept the foundation without question until the occurrence of some monumental scientific achievement produces a noticeable paradigm shift within the community. Such an achievement does not follow the cumulative pattern of science at all, but quite the contrary. In order to account for this noncumulative component of scientific activity, Kuhn formulates a counter-pattern to normal science.

While cumulative science is recognizable by its accordance with the expectations of the community's theoretical framework, Kuhn's counter-pattern originates with the occurrence of a violation of expectations, an anomaly.[18] Either an occurrence in the laboratory does not fall within the scope of the accepted paradigm, or a scientist repeatedly fails to produce a certain result that the paradigm suggests he could. These violations only confirm, says Kuhn, that the world can never quite fit its paradigm-induced version. In this sense, unexpected violations are really gifts to science: they can remind members of the achieved character of their theoretical framework. The anomaly, then, is the conscience of science.

As Kuhn points out, anomalies are always present—even witnessed. But what distinguishes the counter-pattern from Kuhn's cumulative pattern is the willingness of the scientist (few are willing) to pursue the meaning of the anomaly, and then to turn the violation of expectation into a violation of grounds.

According to Kuhn while this second pattern contradicts the normal pattern of scientific self-understanding, it is science nonetheless. If we look at science historically we can discover two traditional modes of scientific work. One relies on theoretical foundations already provided for and structurally tied to a particular scientific community. This is the pattern to which science normally orients itself. The other pattern violates these same foundations while appealing to indexical standards, observations, and formulations created (or re-created) in and for that inquiry, but which are not necessarily tied to any particular scientific community. In fact, the second pattern may completely lack community support. Here, as with the stranger, the tension between the individual and the group emerges most clearly. Kuhn argues that during this counter-mode of scientific inquiry, the scientist involved must formulate a notion of science for himself. He must decide what in his particular scientific community is essential to science and what is not essential and can be discarded.

In contrast, the scientific community (certain representative members), given their commitment to preserving the concrete foundations of their own work, will invariably assert the necessity of every element of that foundation. The community's difference in orientation from that of the iconoclast provides the platform for the struggle that often accompanies the phenomenon of scientific breakthrough.

With regard to these contradictory patterns of science, I use Kuhn's term, "normal science" to refer to the first pattern. Kuhn labels the second pattern "extraordinary research," [19] or alternatively, the work of "creative scientists." [20] I prefer "dialectical inquiry," for the term "dialectic" more closely relates to the phenomenon involved. Dialectic refers to related judgments which on the surface seem mutually contradictory, but when placed within the momentum of a discourse neither cancel each other out nor add up to zero. In other words, while they concretely contradict each other they still display a unity of their own. With regard to the experience of a dialectical transformation in science, we are faced with a situation in which the individual scientist performs what seem to be contradictory practices. He is on the one hand working out a normal scientific problem and, in this sense, is displaying concordance with the interests of the scientific community. On the other hand, he is reconsidering, challenging, and violating the foundations on which normal science rests. While this seems contradictory, it has occurred in the strategies of a number of scientists and therefore is an empirical actuality, a unity of its own. The task, then, in addressing this dialectic would be to approach some understanding of its analytic substance. The dialectical inquiry embraces the contradiction with which it is involved. In this case, it works at normal science while engaging its foundation as a topic of inquiry.

In contrast, normal science seen as a pure type does not make the foundation a matter for discursive concern, not so much because the normal scientist does not want to, but because he cannot experience the relevance of an inquiry into grounds. For him, the pregiven theoretical foundation is relevant only in its taken-for-grantedness. In his functions as scientist, he lives with the support of the community paradigm, but seldom, if ever, will he provide an analytic account of it. The paradigm is of no thematic concern for him (no engaging mystery to him), and never has been from his initial training. Members of the scientific community agree to live within their paradigm-induced world, but do not compel each other to engage its foundation explicitly.[21]

III

The boundedness of intellectual activity in the context of the community that surrounds it is not exclusive to science alone. The activities of art and philosophy are no less delimited when seen within their institutional contexts. Of course all of these activities can produce a significant analytic that distinguishes them markedly from each other. While scientific activity requires members' achievements as preparation and foundation for all succeeding work, the activity of art celebrates its independence from all previous achievements. While scientific activity builds on and continues from its first principles, philosophical activity refers to the necessity of doubting first principles. However, we can also see how the organizing communities function to blur these distinctions.

The radical independence of art, for example, changes concretely in the course of its interchange with the public domain. The creation of a community around a product is synonymous with the beginning of a social evaluation process. No intellectual community makes work public without judging it; in this filtering process, it creates its own sense of tradition by establishing exemplary models of good work. Yet only the product, the most tangible, reproducible element of the work, can ever function securely as a model. Its process and energy remain hidden. Therefore, in its power to judge each item under view, the community can easily relate work to the more tangible but limited features of its exemplary models, but can never guarantee that its judgment derives from the animus, the ground of the work itself. Hence by this process of reification, the community tends to renounce its own potential in favor of its concrete, historically and self-imposed limits, and attempts to hold its members to the requirements of these limitations.

Intellectual breakthrough represents works whose relation to the community changes and can actually betray itself in the process of its own institutionalization. In its capacity to accumulate tradition, the community builds on revolutionary work. But although the original enters the community as resistance, it is then made to function just as the models it first resisted. Members take the concretely reproducible features of the original as their standards and boundaries; the community hides the dialectical momentum of founding works and celebrates their concrete reproduction. Thus the community obscures the difference between the original and its copy, between the critical and the obedient. This occurs in art and philosophy as decisively as it occurs in science—in each instance it is the community that breakthrough must break through.

IV

Using science as the particular setting for his analysis, Kuhn portrays the history of intellectual communities as a series of reawakenings, and each reawakening as a leap of irreducible difference. We must note, however, that for Kuhn the awakening is recognized by its post-revolutionary community. In other words, the actual work of the scientist is not Kuhn's direct reference in defining his topic; rather, the work is admitted as a relevant event for Kuhn only with hindsight, only after it has proven its revolutionary potential and has significantly altered the contours of a segment of the scientific community. Thus from Kuhn's vantage point, Lavoisier discovered oxygen only after the community discovered Lavoisier. Hence Kuhn allows the community to constitute his topic.

This of course need not cause any particular problem for Kuhn, given his commitment to formulate a version of scientific revolution, for the notion of revolution is necessarily tied to its emergence as a community event. Within this framework, however, the discursive event, the breaking through itself, can only be made relevant in the light of the revolution it precedes; it cannot be studied in and for its own telling features. Thus while breakthrough, studied in and for itself, provides an opportunity to address the tension between the individual and the group, Kuhn must shift its axis and admit only that component whose tension is later normalized in the process of institutionalization. Kuhn's breakthrough therefore is limited to what the community relocates within its postrevolutionary boundaries.

If, however, it is the concrete community that breakthrough must break through, we would have to be somewhat suspicious of that community's definition of the topic. Should this same community, recognized for its capacity to limit inquiry, now be invited to outline the limits of its own overcoming? Hardly. In order to formulate a version of intellectual breakthrough centered in itself, we must be able to separate breakthrough from a community's acceptance of it, and address each of these phenomena individually. Kuhn makes no such separation.

Consider, for example, his claim that in science, without a new paradigm there can be no breakthrough: "To reject one paradigm without simultaneously substituting another is to reject science itself." [22] Kuhn formulates this as a rule of science without first demonstrating its necessity. He merely takes his cue from a history of science that is constituted in and by the scientific community. The fact that the community reifies breakthrough is no proof that an inquirer must orient himself to this same process (processing). So, for example, the inquiry that treats not only a particular paradigm but membership itself as a threat must be ruled outside the scope of Kuhn's analysis—and unnecessarily so. Kuhn can show how particular organizing communities constitute a threat to inquiry, but he cannot see their requirement of reconstituting an organizing community as itself an extrinsic limiting feature—a paradigm of its own.

Consider now the adequacy of a second feature of Kuhn's analysis. In his discussion of scientific revolution Kuhn formulates a version of breakthrough[23] in terms of certain generalizable characteristics: the appearance of anomaly in normal scientific work; the extended investigation into the source of the anomaly;[24] the crisis state which emerges for a group of scientists;[25] and the manner in which the new paradigm gains legitimacy and control of relevant segments of their community.[26] However, as Kuhn readily admits, these are not causes of breakthrough in any reasonable sense, nor are they analytic features of it, but merely characteristics which have often accompanied it. He provides little by way of analysis as to what is inherent to the phenomenon of breakthrough itself, saying only that the event "must here remain inscrutable." [27]

But what does it mean for this particular event to "remain inscrutable"? Does the nature of the phenomenon preclude any penetration of itself? Or, given his method of analysis, does Kuhn himself preclude the possibility of such a penetration? We can suspect the latter to be the case, that is, that breakthrough remains impenetrable to Kuhn given the method by which he chooses to organize his discussion. However, to substantiate this suspicion we should formulate an account of why a direct analysis of breakthrough would remain inaccessible to Kuhn.

Intellectual breakthrough is recognizable because of its uniqueness. That is, its major relevance to human inquiry does not lie in those characteristics it shares with other breakthroughs, but in its distinction as an exception. The notion of an "average breakthrough," therefore, is inadequate when compared to the possibilities generated by the phenomenon. Thus an analysis like Kuhn's which organizes the topic around an inventory of shareable features will necessarily rule as extraneous its most relevant dimension—its particularity. A reduction to generalizable characteristics erases the phenomenon's status as an exception. Thus given his commitment to develop a pattern (a typology) of breakthrough, Kuhn is forced to formulate the topic from a position external to it. This chosen orientation binds him to a discussion of the epiphenomenal. If studies in intellectual breakthrough are first kindled and necessitated by the exceptional character of their claimed subjects, then an inquiry into them must sustain their particularity, not merely bury the topic among its generalizables. The topic as formulated, therefore, cannot be permitted to presuppose its subjects completely.

Thus, finding inadequate Kuhn's orientation toward the boundaries of the topic, we find ourselves lingering in the domains of a topical philosophy, in the sense that topical philosophy involves the inquirer in retrieving the fuller regions of the topic.[28] We can conceive of beginning, therefore, with a theme that has been defined and bounded in the commonsense attitude, but whose boundedness we intend to reconsider. The potential depth and breadth of this analysis lies in recognizing a topic that is only partially apprehended in advance.

This of course is how Heidegger begins his analyses. While from the beginning his themes are never entirely visible, nor are his topics ever fully constituted, they can still procure an inquiry and direct Heidegger into that inquiry. For Heidegger, the idea of a topic is that which we have not yet faced, but which we can hope to glimpse through the analysis.[29]

This discussion began with only a partially formulated understanding of intellectual breakthrough. It conceptualized the topic using the following distinctions: its reference to a tension between the individual and the group, its reference to a search for grounds, and the fact that this discursive event surfaces as a challenge to the conventions of the intellectual community's paradigm. But these features do not constitute a decisive formulation of intellectual breakthrough; they do not adequately organize a topic, for they do not adequately bound the phenomenon. They merely generate the concrete beginnings of an inquiry.

At this initial stage of the inquiry then, Freud, Simmel, and Buber provide examples of intellectual breakthrough, but only in terms of a partially formulated topic. An analysis of their work must allow for a reconsideration of the conceptual limits of the topic. We may speak here of a dialectical inquiry whose boundedness is transformed through its examples. Through this analysis, the example is invited to undermine the topic and move it in a certain direction—which of course is only one direction among many. The example may even begin to organize a new boundedness. But all along we should remember that one more analyzed example can always produce—indeed, must always intend—a reconsideration of the boundary.

2
FREUD

I   We could expect that reading a biography of Freud would deepen our understanding of his work. A Freud biography could provide the occasion to confront and reanalyze the psychoanalytic programme; it could provide a series of categories to organize, make transparent and intelligible the momentum of that programme. Indeed, Ernest Jones, in the preface to his three-volume biography of Freud, writes that his most "ambitious" aim is to relate Freud's "personality and the experiences of his life to the development of his ideas." [1] Here Jones assumes the responsibility of analytically tying certain of Freud's biographical data to the center of his ideas, of making the biographical material account for the formation of those ideas. This is a difficult task for any biographer. How Freud's biography can be seen as the seedbed of psychoanalysis is not immediately apparent. If Jones remains faithful to the promise in his preface, he will have to provide for the dialectical relationship that he asserts. That is, in the course of the analysis he will have to weave concrete biographical data into the ideational complex of psychoanalysis.

How does Jones's product relate to the promise in his preface? In the first pages of the biography, Jones develops a portrait of Freud's family in which he contrasts the family's age structure with that of the average Viennese family. He recalls that Freud's father, born in 1815, had already fathered two sons by another marriage before he married Freud's mother in 1855.[2] This resulted in Freud's having two half-brothers as old as his mother. Jones labels this situation "unusual," "confusing" and "complex," and later he uncovers his motive for having alerted us to the theme of the deviant family. He writes, "In tracing, as best we can, the genesis of Freud's original discoveries we may therefore legitimately consider that the greatest of them—namely the universality of the Oedipal complex—was potently facilitated by his own unusual family constellation, the spur it gave to his curiosity and the opportunity it afforded of a complete repression." [3]

In an effort to ground the Oedipal complex, Jones ties it causally to Freud's family structure. Yet how this explanation strengthens our understanding of the Oedipal complex in any way is not apparent. A causal analysis of this sort will always fail to deepen an understanding of a subject because the causal inquirer departs from the subject during the imposed course of the inquiry. Jones looks outside the notion of the Oedipal complex for its cause; the causal—in this case, biographical—explanation is not shown to be inherent to the subject. Jones leaves the topic in order to address the concrete biographical datum which he never elevates to analytic status. If the notions of family complexity and family abnormality are keys to an understanding of this element of Freud's corpus, Jones would be required to find these notions within the Oedipal theme itself. Complexity and abnormality would be the substance of the Oedipal complex. In other words, the theme of complexity and abnormality would provide an entrance into the topic and would enrich our understanding of it. Jones, however, uses this theme as a method of *escaping* the Oedipal topic, never to return to it. This concrete biographical datum remains a tendency with no substance, while the Oedipal complex remains a substance without necessity. It is an item of disembodied knowledge. To quote Hegel, "the tendency is a mere drift which still lacks actuality; and the naked result is the corpse which has left the tendency behind." [4] Jones fails his prefatory promise, not in his effort to reproduce Freud's family age structure, but in his failure to present the rationality whereby the presentation becomes intelligible and relevant.

A second theme that Jones develops in the biography—and one that is central to this study—is that of Freud's estrangement from the scientific community during the years of his most generative insights. This theme is not exclusive to Jones; we find it in Ellenberger's biographical piece,[5] as well as in Freud's letters (specifically the Fliess correspondence),[6] and in his autobiographical works.[7] In fact, we may acknowledge this theme as the most prominent one in the biographies.

Jones and Ellenberger both recall the extraordinarily long period of time that Freud had to wait before being appointed to the rank of Professor Extraordinaire, a title somewhat analogous to Associate Professor.[8] This delay, they mention, was partly due to the reaction of the scientific community to Freud's early work, and partly to the growing anti-Semitic sentiment among high-ranking political figures in Vienna. Jones spends considerable effort outlining the abuse Freud's work suffered among the professionals. He mentions as one instance of this abuse the cold reception given Freud's paper, "The Aetiology of Hysteria,"[9] when Freud presented it before the Society of Psychiatry and Neurology in Vienna in 1896.[10] The editors of the Fliess correspondence recall another instance, a review of Freud and Breuer's book, *Studies in Hysteria*,[11] written by a German neurologist, Dr. Adolf Strumpel (in the *Deutsche Zeitschrift fur Nervenheilkunde*), part of which read as follows: "I do not know whether such fathoming of the most intimate private affairs can in all circumstances be considered legitimate, even on the part of the most high-principled physicians."[12] On this occasion as well as on many others, Freud's biographers assert that the question of Freud's legitimacy as a scientist is a crucial biographical theme. Yet curiously this question too has not excited any concern as a topic of inquiry, which could leave us wondering how this theme has become prominent at all. The rationale for including it has remained an occasion for silence (i.e., it is only there by fiat), and has evaded any reflexive account.

If we accept the importance of the observation that Freud's psychoanalytic investigations were conducted while addressing a hostile scientific community, we should make this our theoretic concern. By addressing the issue of Freud's relationship to the scientific community, we can confront the psychoanalytic programme and restore the rationality of this theme's inclusion into a biographical account of Freud's life. And further, we can show how this theme points to a central tension in Freud's writings.

II

On its most practical level, psychoanalysis is a form of therapy "born out of medical necessity."[13] This therapeutic technique consists of awakening the patient to his own unconscious mental life, and to the relationship between his conscious identity (ego) and the hidden dimensions of human wishes and desires. In a paper entitled "Further Recommendations on the Technique of Psychoanalysis I," Freud describes how he prepares his patients for the psychoanalytic encounter:

> What you tell me must differ in one respect from an ordinary conversation. Ordinarily you rightly try to keep a connecting thread running through your remarks and you exclude any intrusive ideas that may occur to you and any side-issues, so as not to wander too far from the point. But in this case you must proceed differently. You will notice that as you relate things various thoughts will occur to you which you would like to put aside on the ground of certain criticisms and objections. You will be tempted to say to yourself that this or that is irrelevant here, or is quite unimportant, or nonsensical, so that there is no need to say it. You must never give in to these criticisms, but must say it in spite of them —indeed you must say it precisely because you feel an aversion to doing so. Later on you will find out and learn to understand the reason for this injunction, which is really the only one you have to follow. So say whatever goes through your mind.[14]

Speaking "whatever goes through your mind" Freud labels "free association." It is the fundamental rule of his psychoanalytic procedure.

Freud thus instructs the patient that during therapy he must attempt to free himself from the conventional organizing and censoring rules sanctioned by the community. He must disregard the supportive power of the norm (and the law) in an effort to author a speech that authentically represents what goes through his mind. Freud claims that the patient's relationship to the norm (and the law) tends to subvert his authorship, and that his membership in the community interferes with authenticity. The birth of ego coincides with the beginnings of membership in the political sphere. Ego, as one's political identity, finds its direction and support from the community. The community may be characterized by the fact that its organizing of members produces a version of membership as the only dimension of existence. The accepting ego (the unreflective self) submits to this restriction. Ego functions as if membership (existence) were always at stake in one's speech. Ordinary conversation humbles itself to, and thus reinforces, the solidarity of the political organization. Ordinary conversation, as the organizational metaphor for party doctrine, is a method by which ego defends membership.

Ego as political (social) identity, speaks and simultaneously omits.

Thus ordinary conversation, which is ego's vocal life, is characterizable as the simultaneous activities of speaking and omitting. Yet ego does not recognize its own practices, because it does not acknowledge the activity of omission. Instead, for the purpose of maintaining a stable membership, a minute portion of human life is held up as the totality of that life. Ordinary conversation cannot be authentic speech, for what is merely a fragment is presented as the whole. In therapy Freud tries to remove the threat of losing membership. His patients, from the beginning of therapy, must recognize the fragmentary nature of ordinary conversation and of ego itself. The good (receptive) patient addresses ordinary conversation as that which is not to be trusted, and as that to be surpassed. That is, he addresses the coercive nature of his socialization and acknowledges the inauthenticity of his political life.[15]

Science, for Freud, is a metaphor for authenticity. Within the therapeutic encounter, when Freud claims to progress scientifically, he means that he is progressing toward authenticating his patients' speech. And this scientifically produced procedure involves violating restrictive rules imposed on speech (and experience) by the various institutions in which the individual participates. But let us observe that in this context, science is not only a way of authenticating ordinary conversation through debunking the restrictive rules placed upon it. We must acknowledge that science is yet another one of society's institutions with its own rules for ordering and restricting speech. It, too, restrains its participants from speaking whatever goes through their minds. Thus in the same manner that the political sphere interferes with authentic speaking (this particular notion of authentic speaking as speaking "whatever goes through your mind"),[16] the institution of science also interferes with authentic speaking. Furthermore, we should note that science is not isolated from political life in our everyday world.[17] In fact, scientific standards and many scientific findings extensively influence everyday life. Over the last few hundred years, science has gained a position of authority within the wider community, a position previously occupied only by the church. Thus the institution of science does not only rule over the speech of scientists; it has become one of the institutions in our society that directs and controls ordinary conversation. The scientific community has provided the wider community with measures by which all speech, including Freud's, is judged for its authenticity.

This observation reveals a curious problem that must be faced when reading Freud. On the one hand, Freud claims to use science as a method of freeing ordinary conversation from institutional rule. On the other hand, science is itself one of the social institutions that rules ordinary conversation. This paradox was not overlooked by Freud. In his analysis of the Dora case, for example, he frequently refers to the "narrow lines" of legitimate work imposed by his colleagues.[18] In addition his correspondence during the early years of psychoanalysis shows clearly that Freud did experience, more than most members of his generation, the restrictive tendencies of the scientific community.[19] Nothing is more indicative of this than an incident in 1901 when Freud was asked to deliver a lecture on dream theory. Just a few hours before the lecture was to be given, Freud received a letter asking that he illustrate his talk with inoffensive examples, and that he pause before coming to morally objectionable material so that the ladies could leave the room. In a letter to Wilhelm Fliess concerning the episode, Freud wrote, "Such is scientific life in Vienna." [20] Thus while Freud claims to be speaking scientifically, he recognizes conventional, institutional scientific rule as untrustworthy.

It should become evident that Freud does not see his own concrete scientific community as the authentic representative of science. Rather, he feels that he must disregard it as the measure of authentic speech in order to begin to speak authentically.[21]

III

The notion of "free association" points to a distinction between the "good" patient and the "bad" patient, and further clarifies the delimiting influence of society's institutions. The good patient attempts to free himself from conventional institutional rule, while the bad patient organizes his speech with faithful and sole regard for convention. And, as Freud points out, the bad patient's subjugation to the institutions around him prevents him from speaking what goes through his mind.

It should not be difficult to realize that the bad patient is always empirically evidenced as long as there are social institutions that restrain speech. The epitome of the bad patient would be the scientist, for he most clearly organizes his speech in accordance with precise restrictions imposed by the scientific community. We can suggest, then, that with the notions of free association and the good and bad patient, Freud exposes metaphorically the inimical relationship that existed between him and his colleagues. The good and bad patient provide Freud with the occasion to analytically enliven his own estrangement. That is, the scientific community's hostility toward Freud's writings can be seen in terms of the ideational complex of psychoanalysis. The scientific community is criticized for not living up to the mandate of science. It is not being faithful to the intention, the purpose, and the Reason of science, and thus is not authentic. If science had been authentic there would have been no need for psychoanalysis. But science has become the false representative of the scientific ideal. The scientist who speaks only by the rules of the scientific community has constrained himself, has prevented himself from speaking what goes through his mind. Thus, the psychoanalytic corpus can be read metaphorically as criticizing science for having become the perfect exemplar of "repressive" speech.

What kind of operation does the notion of repression describe? In Freud's words, repression is the "corner-stone on which the whole structure of psychoanalysis rests." [22] He writes, "the essence of repression lies simply in turning something away, and keeping it at a distance, from the conscious." [23] Notice, says Freud, that repression cannot dissolve that which it turns away, but can merely keep it in abeyance. Thus the repressed material remains alive. Repression does not interfere with the existence of the material; it interferes with the material's entrance into consciousness, since it is believed that its entrance will disrupt the organization of consciousness. Moreover, because this repressed material remains alive, says Freud, it is always potentially energetic—it remains the omnipresent object of repression. Repression only succeeds by continually expending energy to maintain control over the repressed material. The notion of repression describes a constant animosity between conscious and unconscious: ego is unable to escape what it represses, and its attempt to do so is a predestined failure.

The concrete scientific community, portrayed here as the exemplar of repressive speech, reveals this animosity (most clearly in its relation to Freud's early work). Unable to completely free itself from what it rules as illegitimate speech, the community directs its energy toward repressing that speech which it views as a threat to the stability of the community itself. We may say that with the notion of repression, Freud accuses his colleagues of misdirecting their energy, of concerning themselves solely with the stability of the concrete scientific community, and of elevating that concern above all others. The rules have become confused with the goals, and "working by the rules" has begun to provide its own fascination for the scientists.

Thus normal science, for Freud, has become an icon both for power and sociability. As an icon for power it has turned the Machiavellian ethic of how to rule into a prime purpose of science: scientific speech censors and controls; it takes as its mandate the authority to rule on the legitimacy of other speakers. As an icon for sociability, community maintenance has become a prime activity of community members: the community comes to exist for its own sake rather than for the sake of its work.[24]

Yet Freud shows in his discussion of the nature of repression how speech cannot completely hide repressed material. He points to the mystery of all speech: that even against its will, speech reveals what it has hidden. Seen in the context of our discussion of the scientific community, we can say that scientific speech also reveals its omissions, and that the concrete programme of science can now be approached as the raw material by which to rediscover these omissions. Concrete science retains a memory of its "phylogenetic childhood," [25] a childhood it could never escape.

What is the material that, in repressing, science cannot escape? The repressed material is precisely what animates science in the first place. Freud views the unconscious as a metaphor for the energy that potentiates all productivity of which science is the most prominent example. While science has violated its origins and has lost touch with the power that animates it,[26] the origins remain a vital though hidden dimension of scientific speech, a dimension that presses toward recognition.

Freud's discussion of repression shows metaphorically how a scientific community that turns away from its origins cannot sustain itself indefinitely. The speaker whose speech represses its origins must necessarily carry a burden in his speech—even if ego does not experience it —for inauthentic speech is a burden on the speaker's soul. Freud's theme is to break through the repressive rules of inauthentic speech in order to acquaint each speaker with his own authentic autobiography. The neurotic symptom, then, can be seen as the sign of science breaking down under its own weight, and we may interpret the psychoanalytic programme as designed to meet the crisis of Western science. Thus, Freud's corpus shows how on the one hand science progresses by forgetting its origins, and on the other hand how science must readdress its origins if it is to re-energize itself.

IV

Freud claims to take his energy from science, but disregards conventional scientific authorization to support his programme. The programme is instead supportable by a "science" that Western science no longer remembers. But where does Freud locate this memory? Memory, says Heidegger, is activated in the remembering, in the "gathering and convergence of thought upon what everywhere demands to be thought about first of all." [27] Thus memory is only the remembering of that which is to be remembered. If Freud criticizes science for not remembering, it is not because it cannot report anything of what went before; it is for its failure to remember the essentials. For Freud, what Western science remembers (gathers together into membership) is a false memory, or as he puts it, a "screen memory." [28] As Freud says, a screen memory is an incomplete one in the sense that it does not know why it is remembered. It is unreflexive. The memory does not unify itself with its source. For example, it may produce anxiety for no apparent reason, or it may not produce anxiety the rememberer would think that it should. Thus the screen memory constitutes a partial forgetting and, says Freud, it forgets precisely that which would make the concrete memory intelligible.[29] The screen memory forgets its ground, its Reason. Freud calls these memories "innocent" [30] in the sense that innocence is synonymous with analytic ignorance and thus synonymous with a failure to address essentials.

We can consider Western science innocent in the sense that its memories (its origin, its grounds) are screened. That is, the unity that Western science shows is not a unity with its source, but a concrete unity of members who together turn away from this source. In a number of his works, Freud develops this same theme of the collectivity that comes together precisely for the purpose of turning away from its source. In *The Future of an Illusion*, for example, members unify in order to forget their loss of childhood security;[31] and in *Totem and Taboo*, the brothers unite after killing their father and then organize speech in an attempt to erase this memory—the source of their unity.[32] If science also unifies and simultaneously attempts to erase its memory, where do we locate this memory and thus the essentials of science? Freud claims that memory lies hidden within speech.[33] Therefore the memory of science would be located within scientific speech itself.

Scientific speech points to the excellence of science regardless of whether or not that excellence has been achieved.

This, of course, is not new to Western philosophy. In fact, it is the identical notion with which Plato approaches discourse. Socrates' interlocutors provide instances of false gathering, but Socrates takes the false gathering as the occasion to begin discourse; the false gathering screens true gathering. Discourse, for Plato, is empirical in the sense that it relies on the concrete as the material to elevate and surpass.

While the speech of the scientific community is to be criticized for its failure to be faithful to what animates it, it is to be examined carefully for its memory. That is, concrete science is transformed into the empirical material of analytic discourse. The screen memory is data, the occasion to address the true memory of science. In Freud, scientific speech can be turned back on itself in order to address scientific grounds. Then it would be possible to call out the source of legitimate scientific writing and thus the legitimacy of Freud's authorship. The support for Freud's claim that he speaks scientifically lies hidden within scientific speech. His speech is dialectically tied to the problem of its own legitimacy. It moves toward the hidden life that authorizes the speech and will authorize science itself.

V

This discussion began by describing the psychoanalytic technique of "free association." We found this notion to be inexorably antagonistic to the political sphere, in that it is the political sphere which provides the greatest obstacle to free association. We found also that to an extent, contemporary political life is subject to the standards and judgments of the scientific community. Yet the curious mystery here is that the psychoanalytic encounter calls itself a scientific encounter: science is both the source and the adversary. Therefore, an archeology of the psychoanalytic technique, when read metaphorically, can distinguish between concrete science and its analytic source. It reveals both an attraction and a tension between science (normal science) and the grounds upon which science and all speech rely for their energy. The project of psychoanalysis can be understood as an attempt to move science toward a relationship with this source. Science is to be remembered (analytically reorganized) in order to show its relationship to what owns it. But this distinction is a false one, for science can never truly be distinguishable from its source. The distinction disembodies both normal science and its source and renders them both unintelligible. It only clouds the unity that normal science shares with its source. If the distinction can be accomplished empirically, it is only in an arena where science no longer relates to its source, in a setting where science is a false science. Science can only be true science if it "sources." A science that does not recognize and does not turn toward this unity can never understand why it exists. That science does not understand itself.[34]

Freud's programme, read metaphorically, can be interpreted as an attempt to turn science back on itself and thus to become faithful to itself.[35] True science is to be understood in terms of its faithfulness to what owns it. Thus the question that psychoanalysis can ask is, "How does science science?"

How are we to relate to this question? This question does not create science's sciencing as a tangible form which weighs and grades each particular version of science. It does not wish to preserve science as a fixed subject with a standard set of attributes to which all concrete science appeals for its name and legitimacy. Rather, this question calls science that active subject which comes to life as it sciences.[36] Science sciences in the sense that it "surfaces" [37]—that on every occasion of sciencing it is reborn and reveals its birth. It reexperiences the struggle of its beginning as it participates in that beginning. In his writings Freud often appeals to a return to beginnings when he refers to the "primal" regions of existence. His notions of the "primal scene," [38] "primal phantasy," [39] "primal horde," [40] "primal repression," [41] and primitive fear [42] all bring psychoanalysis to bear on the question of reexperiencing science's beginning. The term "prime" is interesting, for it simultaneously means that which is first, most significant, and essential. Therefore, for Freud, firstness (as beginning) is synonymous with significance and essence. If beginning is understood as being linked to the essential, we should have no trouble grasping the relevance of Freud's search for the beginnings. He formulates the beginning as the analytic center from which all meaning and all movement emanate, and from which all links become structurally intelligible. Primal life captures the whole in the sense that it gives wholeness its meaning.

Freud speaks about "fixation" as the historical moment of primal life.[43] As fixated, this moment comes to possess a lingering, in fact timeless, presence. It is a moment that segregates and collects, and a moment upon which structure is built.[44] Freud asserts that this moment, as beginning and as center, is always the relevant history to return to. The beginning of science, then, can become the focus of the psychoanalytic search. However, the notion of beginning is to be decided by the requirements of an analytic and not by an appeal to any chronological ordering of the events of scientists.[45] Primal science is to be sought only in terms of its being the moment that segregates and collects. In Freudian terminology this moment retains "libidinal energy."

At this point, a brief departure from a direct discussion of the Freud texts is warranted in order to examine a certain formulation of the scientific project in the work of Aristotle. This examination should uncover an analytic beginning of science, that is, a relevant "fixation" in science. Here we must understand the fixed *beginning* as an *end* of a certain movement in the development or evolution of inquiry.[46] I consult Aristotle because in his formulation of the scientific project, a course of inquiry began while, at the same time, other possibilities for inquiry were hidden and subsequently sublimated within the newly arranged "legitimate" scope of science. To uncover this fixation will bring psychoanalysis to bear on the question of the relationship of science to its beginnings.

VI

Aristotle wrestled with the classical Greek form of life to secure a beginning for his new science. This new science is dialectical in its moment of wrestling (discourse), but Aristotle does not reproduce this experience. His new science begins explicitly only after the foundation is secure; he does not treat the securing as an occasion for discourse. When he introduces the basic criteria of this new science, he does so by merely stating what they are. He authorizes their introduction with the claim that these are matters on which all humans agree.[47] For example, at the beginning of the *Metaphysics* he writes, "Such and so many are the notions, then, which we have about Wisdom and the wise," or "we think that knowledge and understanding belong to art," or "we think art more truly knowledge than experience is." [48] In fact, in the first few pages of the *Metaphysics* there may be as many as fifteen such instances which call on the anonymous collective to authorize various notions. This kind of statement would lead us to believe that Aristotle's beginning had been secure long before he began his work. Thus it would seem on the surface that the experience of the birth of Aristotelian science predated Aristotle altogether, and may be found in the classical Greek form of life. Aristotle presents himself as merely an extension of what went before him rather than as the author of a radically new programme. Yet we know from reading Aristotle's predecessors (Plato, Heraclitus, Parmenides) that when he claims that all humans agree, he is not speaking the truth. It becomes clear from reading the classics that all humans do not agree. Plato, for example, would never allow a statement such as "what is called Wisdom [deals] with the first causes and principles of things" [49] to stand preserved and intact in a dialogue. If anything, this statement would only provide him with the occasion to begin discourse, and to display the weakness of speaking in such an unreflexive manner. Then why does Aristotle introduce that statement by appealing to an agreement when there is none? When Aristotle says that all humans agree he is only covering over the radical newness of his programme. This appeal to the stock of commonsense knowledge is a diversion from the ground upon which Aristotle's work does depart from the classics. That is, in his glossing he exempts himself from having to account for his experience of theorizing. The dialectical education, exemplified by the struggle of science's birth, is not given an explicit formulation in the concrete presentation.

However, Aristotle's refusal to address his experience of theorizing should not be construed as an oversight on the part of the author. Rather, it must be understood as a crucial feature of Aristotle's programme which embodies the notion that once a foundation is secured, a science of unlimited progress is possible. A foundation—any foundation—is developed under the requirement that it exist concretely and that its concrete life be stable. For a foundation to exist, it must materialize and defy time (or at least try). It must be concretely grasped and available to anyone at any required moment. Aristotle holds his work to this requirement and thus does not permit himself to make reference to his dialectical struggle with the tradition. Such a reference could only make his foundation a topic of discourse and thereby threaten its concrete preservation. In other words, the foundation may cease to provide a foundation. Thus Aristotle's failure to address it is theoretically conceived and must itself be understood as his experience of theorizing. The newness of Aristotle's science is reflected in its commitment to silence the classical Greek tradition. An explicit engagement with the essence of that tradition will necessarily stand in the way of the new foundation.

Yet Aristotle does consent to refer to the tradition (although only in a casual manner). One such reference appears in the first sentence of the *Metaphysics* when Aristotle writes, "All men by nature desire to know." And later, "For it is owing to their wonder that men both now begin and at first began to philosophize." [50] On these occasions Aristotle seems to be at one with the classical version of theorizing. Desire and wonder are formulated as analytic features of human nature and as the analytic center of philosophizing. In Plato, for example, Desire is philosophical potentiality.[51] Yet while Plato remains involved with this question as that through which human beings struggle toward Wisdom and the Good, Aristotle can only give Desire a few scattered and final references. Moreover, he shows that Desire is not an element of the concrete foundation, for any of Aristotle's references to Desire (wonder) can easily be omitted without in any way harming the foundation.

Yet why does Desire have no place in the foundation when Aristotle himself says that it has a place in the founding? Desire is troublesome for it is not tangible. It presents itself and then leaves. It dies and is reborn. Since it has no formal structure, it cannot be concretely preserved.[52] It cannot give a concrete account of itself. Even when Aristotle mentions Desire, the sentences in which it appears do not display the Desire they speak of. Desire disrupts Aristotle's commitment to move totally into the concrete and to organize a science designed to make the concrete perfectly manageable. In Aristotle, Desire is silenced and thus the dialectic is severed in order to provide for the conquest of the concrete by the concrete. The achievement of beginning science, then, is the achievement of neglecting its analytic referent for practical reasons. In Freudian terminology, this is an action of orientation toward the "reality principle."

The development of the reality principle, says Freud, is each human being's accomplishment. Given a natural human dependence upon things and thingness, the concrete world holds the power to demand the alteration of primal life.[53] Thus a new set of obligations is imposed. Attention, which had once been the expression by which human freedom voiced its desire, now becomes tied to the senses which can only provide for a relationship with concreteness. Concreteness is given the accent of reality (of its participation in Being), but at the neglect of Desire's participation in Being. Thus the development of the reality principle marks the victory of the concrete over fantasy, imagination, and myth. Truth becomes a metaphor for "at-one-ness" with concrete life and no longer appeals to the voice of Desire.

In his beginning of science and the scientific structure, Aristotle codifies this "natural" dependence upon concrete objects and provides it with an overwhelming respectability. While philosophy was once the struggle to elevate ourselves through and beyond concreteness, Aristotle accepts the failure to move beyond concreteness as the starting point of all future discourse. Ordinary life is now the standard which cannot be surpassed. This failure of ordinary life is now legitimate and "human nature," as the rationalization for this failure, becomes the watchword of all those who wish to turn their attention away from the Sun with the sole interest of making the Cave a more comfortable place in which to live.

Freud's notion of the reality principle gives him the occasion to wonder what is involved in the management of the concrete. By showing the supersession of the reality principle as a practical accomplishment, Freud is able to transcend this monopolistic attention to concreteness. His discovery allows him to look deeply into humanness and human nature to point to the philosophical potentiality residing within. The manner in which this potential surfaces is the crucial import and significance of psychoanalysis.

VII

In the generic text of psychoanalysis, *The Interpretation of Dreams*,[54] Freud takes dream reports as an occasion to contest and interpret human speech. This occasion does not remain a simple struggle to achieve the correct interpretation of particular dream reports. Freud is not exclusively concerned with correct description. Rather, the significant import of this text is Freud's notion of interpretation which constitutes a challenge to the established limits of the hermeneutic field.

In *The Interpretation of Dreams*, dream reports are used to chart an area of double-meaning expression. Speech possesses both manifest and hidden meanings. For Freud, while any speech functions to allow ego to maneuver within its concrete world, this same speech is also a disguised version of human expressiveness. What human beings really wish to express and must express as part of their nature, is hidden within speech. Speech possesses a plurivocity of meaning, direction, and intention and thus becomes a rich beginning point of analysis. But Freud's challenge to the established hermeneutic field is directed most specifically toward a scientific community in which disguised speech and plurivocal language have no analytic status. Recall in the *Metaphysics* Aristotle's directive: "Not to have one meaning is to have no meaning." [55] Aristotle limits speech to unequivocal expression. This hints at a conception of speech as solely the tool of concrete life. Recall how Aristotle brings the foundation of science to permanence by extracting and ignoring its unstable elements (Desire). Similarly for Aristotle, language must be molded into a precise instrument by severing any connection with sources of instability. In order for science to manage the concrete world, its language must itself be manageable. Aristotle transforms language into a scientific tool; as such, it can no longer be an arena of interpretation. In science, the study of language becomes the mechanistic search for precision without regard for how the notion of precision became the overriding authority. For Aristotle, hiddenness and plurivocity constitute a failure of speech rather than an integral feature of it. For Freud, however, hiddenness and plurivocity provide speech with its vitality. Thus the Freud corpus chastizes scientific speech for its failure to see its subject as much more expressive than it imagines, and for its failure to recognize and turn toward its own expressiveness.

VIII

Nietzsche uses the phrase "clucking of tongues" to refer to the unreflective speech of the crowd. [56] But to call "Other's" speech "clucking" is a method of holding Other at a distance and dismissing his speech altogether. Nietzsche calls the voices in the crowd "clucking" and at once orients to the crowd's speeches as perfectly shallow, as hiding no philosophical potential. But for Freud even the "clucking of tongues" shares of the essence of humanness, in the sense that humanness lies hidden within it. Even the voices of the "herd" hide articulate expression. For Freud the "clucking of tongues" calls out for psychoanalytic encounter as does all speech. Clucking is false speaking, but falseness is not to be understood as not possessing truth. False speech is speech that is spoken while its truth is unthought. [57] The false speaker is the speaker who does not hear the truth that he speaks. All speech shares in the expressive potential of speech; true and false speaking are ways of referring to a distinction between speech that hears its own truth and speech that does not. In Freud the difference between "clucking" and articulate speech dissolves in order to capture a higher unity of which they both partake. The problem of the expressiveness of language is not a matter of devising different words and speeches, but of orienting to the same words in a different way. Freud imparts the voices of the "herd" with a tragic, unfulfilled eloquence and makes all speech the potential starting point of discourse.

How does this expansion of the hermeneutic field manifest itself? Freud converts unequivocal speech into symbolism, providing analytic status to the symbolic life of speech. With this provision, he directs us toward the symbolic function in science.

For speech to be symbolic means that it shares in two lives. First it possesses a manifest meaning which finds its life in the concrete world. This manifest meaning constitutes an orientation toward precision and unequivocal expression. The tension of its life is a pull in the direction of closure and systematization. The manifest meaning, however, covers a hidden voice which constitutes the second life of symbolism. The voice that lies underneath this literal and immediate meaning of the symbol is not even language in a concrete sense. It is a voice of our pre-articulate nature. It is unable to surface as words and must attach itself to something which can surface. When it does surface, it remains hidden. That is, it announces itself indirectly because language does not possess the power to formulate it explicitly. Thus the symbol, born out of the limitation of language (the "reality principle" is Freud's metaphor for this limitation), functions both to cover and reveal meaning ("sublimation" is Freud's metaphor for the symbolic function of covering and revealing). Within the symbolic attitude, the manifest meaning is seen as a covering-over, a manipulation in tune with the demands of concreteness; yet it excites and invites a dis-covering, a letting out of the richness of hidden meaning. Says Ricoeur, "Symbols give, they are the gift of language; but this gift creates for me the duty to work, to inaugurate philosophic discourse." [58]

To forget the symbolic life of speech is to be lazy, for it is to be cognizant only of the speech that covers and not of what the cover covers over. Lying hidden within speech is the vast domain of human desire. Freud's unconscious is a reflection of and upon Desire and an attempt to allow Desire to surface. Desire surfaces in all speech, given our commitment to struggle with speech and to make it philosophically powerful. Concrete speech, for Freud, is always prior to and the substance of inquiry.

Given this notion and given our metaphoric reading of psychoanalysis as an analysis of scientific speech, one can argue that the Freud corpus castigates normal science for being lazy, for not recognizing its speech as symbolic, and thus for not exposing Desire. Desire's inability to surface permanently in a concrete setting has been translated by normal science as failure. For Freud, however, this inability is precisely the way in which Desire secures its immortality. In a concrete setting it can be altered or destroyed; but in its hiddenness it retains its energy as the source of all human productivity. Freud calls on science to recognize this hiddenness, that is, the hermeneutic that makes hiddenness lively.

IX

I have suggested that Freud's writings can be read metaphorically as an analysis of the relationship between normal science and its source. To support this suggestion I have argued, first, that some of Freud's life-experiences regarding his relationship to the scientific community invite such a reading, and second, that the Freud corpus lends itself very easily to this metaphor. However, we must make the following observation. We know that Freud seldom misses an opportunity to apply psychoanalytic precepts beyond the practical concerns of therapy. He uses psychoanalysis in discussions of literature,[59] art,[60] politics,[61] law,[62] and religion.[63] Science, however, escapes such treatment. At no time does Freud take science and scientific speech as an occasion to uncover a hidden psychological complex of motives and desires. Thus the question must be asked that if Freud exempts science as a topic of inquiry, by what rule do I suggest one read his corpus metaphorically as an inquiry into science?

In *The Future of an Illusion*, an interesting discussion takes place with reference to this question. Recall that in this book Freud characterizes religion and religious self-understanding as an illusion, and writes that religious doctrine and the concrete religious community surface in an attempt to cover certain universal psychological conflicts. During the presentation of his argument, Freud occasionally interrupts his discussion in order to anticipate possible criticisms from his readers. On one such occasion he asks that if religion constitutes a covering over and a denial of its own grounds, can the same also be said of politics and science? Freud answers affirmatively and adds that such an analysis "would not be wasted." [64] In the area of politics we can see that Freud did further analysis. His *Civilization and Its Discontents* and his open letter to Einstein, "Why War?", both provide glimpses of a psychology of politics.[65] However, in the area of science no such analysis was forthcoming. This observation leads to the following question: Why does Freud not treat science as a topic when his life experiences invite such treatment, when his corpus lends itself to the topic, and when he himself acknowledges the possibility and the value of such an analysis? We can only assume that it was through no accident that science and scientific speech escape analytic treatment. Clearly, Freud avoided the topic.

However, this act of avoidance parallels the act of avoidance discussed earlier with reference to Aristotle's initiation of the scientific paradigm. When Aristotle brings science to permanence by hiding its origins in Desire, he extracts from philosophical inquiry its prime source of instability and thus can provide a concrete foundation, a stable support for scientific investigation. All further normal scientific research can appeal to this foundation as the concrete source of its own security and stability. Of course as a consequence of using science as a support, normal science cannot explicitly engage its foundation in discourse.

In his avoidance of science as a topic, Freud reestablishes this same commitment to Aristotle's paradigm. Psychoanalysis, in its capacity as a practical therapeutic procedure, requires a certain stability to be useful within the concrete world. Given this requirement, Freud organizes psychoanalysis under the supportive power of science and thus can appeal to science in his effort to achieve stability for this practical programme. As such, Freud accepts the limitation imposed upon scientists not to explicitly engage the tradition in discourse; he agrees to repress science's origins in Desire. However, unlike most scientists, Freud is unable to bury Desire altogether, for Desire is precisely that which has been discovered (rediscovered) through psychoanalysis. Thus Freud can only agree to avoid explicitly uncovering hidden Desire within the work of science. But he remains committed to exposing hidden Desire in every other aspect of social life. As a result, a discussion of the relationship between normal science and its source must be relegated to metaphor in order to preserve the concrete significance of psychoanalysis. In other words, as a practical therapeutic procedure, psychoanalysis cannot invite a discussion of its own hidden desire, nor can it invite an analysis of the symbolism of its own speech. Such a discussion could only disrupt the use of psychoanalysis within the domain of therapy. Thus Freud avoids the one topic that could encourage inquiry into the grounds of his work, and he hides this tension beneath the manifest discussion of psychoanalysis.

Freud's corpus, then, marks a breaking through to a new science whose focal point is the symbol. It is a science that explores its own sources in human desire while at the same time attempting to preserve the concrete programme of science as a source of practical knowledge. The symbol is the nexus of concrete and analytic life. Freud's orientation to symbolism provides a way to protect the Aristotelian programme while simultaneously exposing the violence it can do to the human soul. That is, Freud attempts to preserve the hiddenness of Desire while also recognizing Desire as hidden. His new science displays the tension of science's sciencing as a dialectic—as a moving in the direction of concreteness while always remembering and regenerating its analytic tie to Desire. In this sense only does science show its roots in, and live in, Western philosophy.

3
SIMMEL

Kuhn characterizes scientific paradigms as achievements which provide new orientations to one or many areas of scientific work, and which isolate limited sets of problems to be investigated and limited ways of formulating those problems. When a sector of the scientific community accepts the authority of a paradigm, says Kuhn, members' attention is directed solely toward that set of problems that the paradigm defines. At the same time, that particular sector rules as illegitimate or uninteresting all work that does not proceed from the paradigm. Thus while the scientific community awakens certain possibilities among its members, it also restricts— even hides—other possibilities.

As I mentioned in chapter one, Kuhn shows how occasionally a scientist experiences the violence of these restrictions in the course of his work and begins to reconsider the grounds of the accepted paradigm. He finds it necessary to violate the paradigm's authority if he is to proceed with the work in which he is involved. But as I also mentioned, breakthrough, for Kuhn, not only involves overcoming restrictions imposed by the accepted paradigm, but also involves formulating a new paradigm and its acceptance within a sector of the scientific community. Thus from Kuhn we derive the notion—commonly held with reference to the scientific, philosophical, and artistic communities— that without a new paradigm there can be no breakthrough. This particular notion, however, can restrict our ability to deal with what is most relevant in the phenomenon of breakthrough. In my study of Freud, I found no reason to question this notion, for Freud's career exemplifies the structure that Kuhn outlines. However, applying this structure to every moment of intellectual breakthrough would result in a misapprehension of the deeper relevance of certain other authors. The following studies will examine two authors—Georg Simmel and Martin Buber—for whom this structure itself constituted tacit restrictions to be broken through in the course of their work.

This chapter treats the career and writings of Georg Simmel, the German sociologist-philosopher. If Simmel's significance were to be measured in terms of his power to attract followers to a new paradigm, he must be considered a virtual failure. Not only did he not attract a wide following to a new paradigm, but Simmel's audience was not convinced that he worked within a paradigm at all. With Kuhn's particular requirement of breakthrough, it is a mystery why Simmel's work is even included among the monuments of sociological thought. Yet, I have chosen to discuss Simmel precisely in order to question Kuhn's notion of breakthrough. One purpose of this study is to approach an analytic version of breakthrough that transcends the solely concrete theme of status within the community. Can we formulate Simmel's work as having achieved scientific breakthrough, and can breakthrough emerge independent of the struggle for supremacy within a community?

This formulation will begin by presenting and analyzing the criticisms leveled at Simmel by his colleagues with respect to his non-paradigmatic orientation; then it will show how Simmel's major contribution to sociological-scientific thought may be seen in terms of his having anticipated these criticisms, and in terms of his having radically reinterpreted their source of authority. In doing this he tacitly formulates a new version of scientific membership and forces us to reconsider Kuhn's conception of breakthrough.

I

Simmel's writings were, and still are, received by the scientific community with a noticeable degree of ambivalence. In one respect, his work was clearly interesting or fascinating—perhaps even brilliant, for Simmel provided a rich source of new formulations and stimulating observations. Yet somehow his work was often seen as contemptible.

To Emile Durkheim, the father of scientific sociology and Simmel's contemporary, it displayed no clear system of orientation.[1] It was fragmented, with "no connection" from one piece to the next.[2] Pitirim Sorokin writes that Simmel's work "results in a series of logical inconsistencies, and in a vagueness of theoretical constructions."[3] Yet even those who greatly admired and were clearly influenced by Simmel's work could not overlook its fragmentary character, its apparent lack of any clear system. Max Weber, who in one comment calls Simmel's writings "simply brilliant" and says "nearly every one of his works abounds in important new theoretical ideas and most subtle observations,"[4] cannot hide his antagonism toward the fragmentary character of the work. He labels the methodology "unacceptable" and the manner of presentation "strange" and "uncongenial."[5] Leopold von Wiese, who may be considered a formal disciple of Simmel, also takes issue with this one unacceptable trait. He refers to the "lack of transition from one [thought] to another" as a "disadvantage intimately linked with the essence of his thought."[6] Thus for those who like Simmel's work as well as for those who do not, the criticism remains the same. The work is unbounded, fragmented, unsystematic.[7]

Yet, what is most curious about this criticism is that Simmel's critics feel no obligation to formulate the standard by which they criticize his work. They recognize fragmentation or disunity as such negative characteristics in scientific work that no further explanation is required. In other words, since objectively visible unification is considered a fundamental necessity of scientific work, fragmentation is by its very nature a failure. However, let us try to understand the sense in which the critics consider fragmentation synonymous with failure. This will help us understand more fully the grounds upon which normal science rests, the grounds of the community upon which Simmel participates as an author.[8] More important, it may begin to uncover the manner in which Simmel does participate. This has always been a mystery to his audience.

Lewis Coser, who edited a book of commentary on Simmel, conceives of fragmentation in the following manner: "Simmel was never tempted by the esprit de systeme. Whether from impatience or from sheer inability to concentrate for any length of time on a particular problem, he moved from one topic to the next, from one line of reasoning to another."[9] Here Coser characterizes the failure of fragmented writing in psychological terms, as indicative of a certain negative character trait. Since Simmel lacks the necessary patience to perform the kind of strictly disciplined work that science demands, he is not fit to be a scientist.[10] This particular criticism is traditional in the social science community. Durkheim, for example, in his effort to initiate a scientific paradigm for sociology, formulates this same notion in the preface to *The Rules of Sociological Method:* "if there is to be a social science, we shall expect it not merely to paraphrase the traditional prejudices of the common man but to give us a new and different view of them. . . . The reader must bear in mind that the ways of thinking to which he is most inclined are adverse, rather than favorable, to the scientific study of social phenomena; and he must consequently be on his guard against his first impressions." [11] Here Durkheim provides for a distinct separation of scientific thinking from everyday thinking on the basis of a difference in quality. Scientific thinking is more trustworthy than ordinary thinking due to its meticulous processing. In contrast, ordinary thinking is not mediated by a thorough processing of the contents of thought. In fact, ordinary thinking, which Durkheim points out is inclined toward "first impressions," is hardly processed at all.[12] It is lazy thinking. Thus for Durkheim as well as for Coser, Simmel's work fails. Science is formulated as a standard of excellence, and fragmentation, which they find in Simmel's work, becomes a metaphor for laziness.

Durkheim provides a further rationale behind authorizing science as a standard of excellence. Only within a "methodically disciplined" [13] attitude, he says, can the science of sociology materialize as a collective intellectual activity. In an article on Simmel, Durkheim writes that "we must accurately isolate social facts and must show what it is that forms their unity in order to avoid reducing sociology to nothing but a conventional label applied to an incoherent agglomeration of disparate disciplines." [14] And further, "while pretending that it defines research, . . . [Simmel's work] actually leaves it to the fancy of the individual." [15] We see then that for Durkheim, if scientists were not "methodically disciplined," the doing of sociology would not lead to the formation of a unified discipline.[16] Sociology would refer concretely to some scattered individuals who have nothing at all to do with one another. Thus the unity that Durkheim attempts to form in isolating social facts is not simply the unity of social facts, but also the unification of sociologists. The isolation of social facts becomes the mutual activity of practicing sociologists and thus the unifying mechanism within the sociological community. For Durkheim, all sociologists must work within a single, disciplined framework; without such a framework, their speech would be indistinguishable from ordinary, everyday speech. Durkheim judges Simmel's work on the basis of its inability to unify sociology. For Durkheim, then, science means living according to a community-sponsored paradigm.

But what is the purpose of this unified collective and why can we not "leave things to the fancy of the individual"? Durkheim's intention in overruling the natural diversity of practitioners is to secure a one-ness, a uniformity for the fruits of sociological investigation. Given the same orientation to the acquisition of knowledge, he hopes that some agreement will be reached in explanations of the social world. Thus Durkheim organizes sociological work independently of individual fancies in order to negotiate a corpus of secure, trustworthy, and objective knowledge.[17] The disciplined unification of sociologists provides a ground for the structural unification of sociological knowledge. Practitioners must agree once and for all to embrace this model of sociological work; but implicit here is an agreement no longer to expend energy questioning and debating its underlying, achieved character. Although discourse may transpire within the confines of this newly structured paradigm, members are encouraged not to address the grounds of the paradigm itself.

Simmel, as an outsider, a stranger[18] to this "methodically disciplined" framework, recalls other possibilities for inquiry. As such he reminds members of the achieved character of the unified collective and threatens the euphony of the Durkheimian enterprise. The fragmentary, unsystematic character of his work makes reference to Simmel's reluctance to fit into this or any objectively disciplined framework. In this context, Simmel is seen as the enemy of concerted inquiry, and fragmentation becomes a metaphor for nihilism and intellectual anarchy.

Von Wiese, in his critique of Simmel, supports this idea, but not for the purpose of strengthening the Durkheimian project. Rather, he attempts to reformulate Simmel's corpus into a concretely unified paradigm of its own: "But it seems to me that this science of the forms of association is in need of certain guiding ideas—of a unified goal—if it is to proceed from repeated analyses to the attainment of a concluding synthesis. This is especially true of Simmel's work: as far as I can tell, his investigations run the danger of ending in scattered fragments." [19] For von Wiese, a work requires underlying, guiding statements, but not simply in order to produce a necessary outline for others to follow—which is what Durkheim would argue—but to ensure the concrete survival of the work. Guiding principles make the work easily tangible. A work that is reducible and then concretely reproduced in one rather neat package cannot be easily misplaced. Simmel's work fails, argues von Wiese, in its refusal to lend to reduction, with the result that some or even many of Simmel's valuable insights could easily be lost, or end in "scattered fragments." For von Wiese, fragmentation shows the work's groundlessness and lack of endurance, and is the sign of the work's probable mortality.

Thus among the various comments and criticisms regarding Simmel's work, a certain rationality emerges. It expresses an attitude that "true" scientific activity occurs only through the consolidation of a unified paradigm within the scientific community. This rationality shows itself concretely in the continuous concern for systematization and reduction to primary guiding statements. Given this expressed concern, scientific work is judged adequate only in terms of its correspondence to the achieved direction of the scientific community. Simmel does not fully share this attitude; his work contributes neither to the achievement of a unified collectivity nor to its concrete preservation over time. As such, he is judged as having failed to meet the "high standards" of membership in the scientific community.

Yet, is science necessarily synonymous with this version of the scientific community? Does doing science in this way respond fully to the essential nature of science? Is the source of this particular version of science fully integrated with the source of science? And is a scientific community of strict concrete grounding and unidirectional expression the only arena in which science can manifest itself? How would Simmel respond to these concerns?

II

Prominent among the various themes discussed by Simmel is the distinction between the concepts of "individual" and "group member." [20] He distinguishes these two concepts in that the individual must undergo a transformation of sorts in the course of group participation. Simmel says that group members relate to one another on the basis of what is communally intelligible. What is not communally intelligible, yet what may constitute an element of an individual's personality, must be withheld or denied by him during his participation within the group. The group encourages its members to participate in the life of the group (in its ideals and aspirations) to the extent that in their life as members they may become the microcosmic embodiment of the group's personality. The member is encouraged to display for the group only those personality elements that are relevant to group life. In this way, a member's personality emerges as distinct from the individual's personality. We may interpret this as the price of membership: the group member sacrifices all that is not communally intelligible. But this is not to say that the group member necessarily participates half-heartedly. Simmel does not intend here to characterize the attitude that an individual carries into group life. In fact, a member's attitude may be totally absorbed with feelings of identification. Whether he participates wholeheartedly or halfheartedly does not negate the fact that *only a fragment of his whole self participates*. Group membership is made possible, says Simmel, by the capacity of the individual to "decompose" his personality into fragments.[21] The group member is always a fragment of the individual.

Consider this formulation with reference to the scientific community represented above by Durkheim, von Wiese, Coser, and Weber—some of its most respected members. In this community the achievement of collective life is a more careful procedure than in most groups. During the many years that constitute an adequate scientific training, a radical transformation of the individual is called for. The individual must develop a carefully refined fragment of his personality and learn to express only that fragment, which purposely coincides with the foundation and direction of the concrete scientific community. Fragmentation of personality is the requirement of membership in any group, but in the scientific community in which Simmel participates, it is accomplished with a certain efficiency and precision. While the decision to join this community may enable a member to perfect and articulate a certain fragment of his personality, it also restricts his ability to express the remainder of his personality.

Simmel's formulation of the process of participation within groups enables him to introduce a curious tension into the notion of fragmentation. We recall that his work was judged fragmentary for its failure to provide a systematic unity believed necessary among scientists. But Simmel argues that this achievement of an objectively visible collective unity (the achievement of a unified paradigm) is only possible given the fragmentary participation of members. With this tension, a dialogue concerning priorities emerges between Simmel and representatives of the scientific community. Simmel takes the concept "individual" as a unity of its own in order to label the participation of scientists as fragmentary, while the scientific community takes its achieved unity as the standard by which to judge Simmel's work as fragmentary. The argument over priorities is concerned with which vantage point represents the highest ideal. Simmel argues that science has perfected one segment of personality at the expense of the others, while representatives of the scientific community argue that Simmel submitted too easily to every individualistic whim of his personality, and as a result, perfected very little. It is in the context of this argument that Simmel discusses the relative values of both the fragment that is visible within the collectivity and the fragment that remains the private property of the individual.

According to Simmel, elements of personality that are communally intelligible are necessarily those which are most diffuse. Moreover, in that those elements are the possessions of many, it must be easier to possess them. Thus, they must be elements which are intellectually inferior.[22] Conversely, qualities that are intellectually superior are possessed by a few or perhaps by only one individual, and as such, do not emerge within the collectivity. The collectivity calls out to the lower elements of its members, since this is what most humans share, while it denies the higher ones. Thus Simmel locates the grounds of the highest intellectual achievement as the unique unity of the individual. In other words, the individual is the source of the highest intellectual standard.

This identical theme finds a voice in the work of Nietzsche, although in a tone that expresses the tremendous anger of this lonely philosopher. For example in a portion of *Thus Spoke Zarathustra*, sarcastically entitled "On the New Idol," Nietzsche writes of the "state, where the slow suicide of all is called 'life'.... Where the state ends—look there." [23] Only in the spaces between, where the state does not intervene or interfere, does Nietzsche find the rare moments of human intellectual achievement. For Nietzsche as well as for Simmel, the collectivity does not constitute the fulfillment of the higher human qualities, but of the lower.

III

Simmel discusses the positive side of fragmentation in his article, "The Adventure." [24] We speak of an adventure, says Simmel, as an experience of special quality quite distinct from our other experiences and thus separated from the continuity of our lives. The adventure is an extracted fragment, tied to our lives with "fewer threads" than are ordinary experiences.[25] While portions of our lives are formed and recognized by what went before and what comes after and thus automatically fit into the flowing continuity of befores and afters, the adventure does not. Its beginning and end are functions of its own character. The contents of the adventure alone determine where the adventure begins and where it ends. The very character of this fragment is dependent on its being isolated.

Since the adventure is dependent on its isolation, it exists with little reference to what lies outside of it. It thus can count on minute support from the rest of life. The structure and continuity of everyday life are weakened and the individual is left without a stable orientation. Why? Because the adventure originates precisely out of an inability to experience something "in the same old way." Whether out of a change in contents or out of some feeling of necessity or both, we sacrifice the comfort of a continuous and uninterrupted life. This may be conceived of as a negative quality of the fragmented experience (perhaps in the same sense that von Wiese spoke about "ending in scattered fragments"), or it may be considered a positive quality depending on the adventure's outcome. Still, during the adventure, the outcome (the coming out) is of little relevance, so its positive and negative characteristics are not experienced in themselves. What is experienced is the excitement of chance. Chance, which constitutes the unity of positive and negative, becomes a feature of the adventure's teleological framework.[26] It comes to be sought for its own sake, regardless of outcome. Within the excitement of the adventure, this unity of positive and negative, as chance, comes to take on a totally positive character. Thus, adventure is characterized by its integration with chance, danger, and risk, and these are precisely what constitute its excitement.

While adventure holds the possibility of failure and destruction, it also holds the possibility of the "highest gain." [27] Gain, in this sense, comes not only from the passion that centers within the experience, but also from experiencing the contents of the adventure in their naked form, uninhibited and unaltered by the motives of everyday life.[28]

This direct experience of contents is intimately linked with another feature of the adventure. When Simmel writes that the adventure is attached to everyday life with "fewer threads than are ordinary experiences," he is defining more than the adventure's relationship to its surroundings. He is also referring to an important element of the adventure's form: its wholeness. Recall that the contents alone determine where the adventure begins and ends, and that much of the structure, motive, and continuity of surrounding life are suspended. Yet, if the structure does not come from outside, it must be manufactured from within as an integral commitment of the experience itself. In other words, the adventure molds its own structure. In the sense of this commitment, self-sufficiency can emerge in a fragment. This is not to say that a fragment is necessarily self-sufficient (recall von Wiese's warning about "ending in scattered fragments"). Certainly a fragment can remain without a meaning or a center that will give it substance. In the adventure, however, this need not be the case. For while it separates itself from the center of life and appears to exist "entirely beyond life," somehow, "if by a long and unfamiliar detour" it reorients itself to that center.[29] Says Simmel, "Indeed, it is an attribute of this form to make us feel that in ... the adventure the whole of life is somehow comprehended and consummated." [30] The notion of the "adventure" expresses a special commitment to unity, for in this fragment lies the experience of unity itself.

Given the notion that the adventure forms its own unity, we may say that each adventure constitutes a beginning in the sense that beginnings are the product and the achievement of a new experienced unity. In *The Scientific Intellectual*, Lewis Feuer suggests that this same phenomenon characterizes the beginning of modern science.[31] Feuer shows how the adventurous ethic was an integral feature of modern science, when in its beginning it first captured its independence and structure (unity) and surfaced concretely. We may inquire, however, whether this adventurous ethic has been neglected within the scientific community as a direct consequence of paradigmatic unity. Surely the scientific community displays a certain unity, but does it ever experience this unity? Or are the requirements of this unity merely passively and thoughtlessly met? In other words, does science suppress adventure as the result of the risk involved? In the adventure, characterized by its willingness to risk the loss of unity, unity is reconsidered, violated, and perhaps recaptured.

When Simmel discusses the professional adventurer as a human being to be admired, he does not want us to conceive of this individual only as one who swims long distances or climbs mountains. The career adventurer may also be the adventurous scientist who, relying on his own strength, violates the support of the community paradigm and makes an adventure of each scientific experience. It is characteristic that even after this individual captures unity, he must leave it in order to relocate it elsewhere. For him, unity is only authenticated when it is experienced. To hold onto the same unity and attempt to preserve it concretely would only mean that he would be present to witness its decay. It is not as important for him that each fragment of his work be the extension of the concreteness of a paradigm and that all of his work be intelligible in terms of this paradigm; it is more important that each fragment be an adventurous occasion that reconsiders its foundations and struggles toward the source from which unity arises.

IV

All the topics that Simmel concerns himself with are related in some manner to the dialectical tension between the individual and the group, that is, the dimensions of the human struggle for individuality. Whether the topic is subordination, the poor, the character of eighteenth-century thought, or the adventure, Simmel almost always expresses some concern for this theme. It should not surprise us then that this theme constitutes Simmel's personal orientation to inquiry, that his writing becomes the medium through which he experiences the tension between himself and his community, and the medium through which he struggles for his individuality.

By uncovering the potentially positive nature of fragmentation in the character of the adventurer, Simmel offers us the key to the stylistic import of the Simmelian corpus. Fragmentation does not necessarily imply failure, although it may; nor is it merely a stylistic quirk with little relation to the contents of the work. In the case of Simmel's writings, and by virtue of his topical concern with the theme of fragmentation, it points us toward a particular conception of theorizing that is characteristic of Simmel's intellectual commitment. He not only presents a concrete formulation of the dialectical tension between the individual and the group; he shows this tension to be alive in his writing. Thus Simmel's fragmentary style may suggest that he experienced each occasion of writing as synonymous with the struggle to be free from any one particular structure or foundation. Kurt Wolff writes, in his introduction to *The Sociology of Georg Simmel*, "Simmel often appears as though in the midst of writing he were overwhelmed by an idea, by an avalanche of ideas, and as if he incorporated them without interrupting himself, digesting and assimilating only to the extent granted him by the onrush." [32] For Simmel, no paradigm is more compelling than the theorist's receptivity toward the experience of theorizing. For him, the community's paradigm often operates as a severe constraint. If Simmel's work is fragmented, it is as a consequence of his relationship with the contents of thought. In *Soziologie* he formulates this same notion as follows:

> If I myself stress the wholly fragmentary, incomplete character of this book, I do not do so in order to protect myself, in a cheap manner, against objections to this character. For when measured by the ideal of objective perfection, the selection of the particular problems and examples contained in this work doubtless presents a haphazard character. Yet if this character should strike one as a defect, this would only go to prove that I have not been able to clarify the fundamental idea of the present volume. For according to this idea, nothing more can be attempted than to establish the beginning and the direction of an infinitely long road—the pretension of any systematic and definitive completeness would be, at least, a self-illusion. Perfection can here be obtained by the individual student only in the subjective sense that he communicates everything he has been able to see. [33]

It is in this sense that Simmel's work achieves its dialectical character. His theme of the dialectic between the individual and the group cannot emerge (cannot make its presence felt) simply by Simmel's writing about it concretely within the corpus. Talking about the dialectic is not tantamount to producing it. The dialetic can only surface when its tension also surfaces as an integral feature of the speech. [34] In this way, Simmel's adventuring nature and thus his resulting fragmented style become the grammar of his dialectic. Moreover, with the adventurous spirit as itself an occasion of the dialectic's tension, we can suggest that Simmel provides the grounds by which we can conceptualize a work's authenticity. We can distinguish between true and false speech on the basis of whether or not the speech is contained in the life of the speaker. That is, the speech can be seen as being tested in the character and actions of the speaker. The initial question to ask is not so much whether or not we agree with Simmel's content, but whether or not Simmel should be the one presenting it. Thus what surfaces here concretely as style is really a conception of authentic speech as speech that is spoken honestly. Only in this manner is the dialectical character of the speech achieved—when the speech (theory) and the life of the speaker (practice) share an intimate relationship.

In the introduction to his commentary, *Georg Simmel*, Coser discusses Simmel's "dialectic of social life." [35] He characterizes the dialectic in terms of the "ambivalence" of social life and the unity of "harmony and disharmony" in social relations. Yet Coser fails to grasp the essential nature of dialectical thought. At one point in the introduction, in speaking about Simmel's final work *Lebensanschuung: Vier metaphysische Kapitel*,[36] Coser writes, "It was not granted to Simmel to solve the tensions and contradictions with which he grappled throughout his life." [37] What Coser does not realize is that dialectical thinking is precisely an attitude in which "tensions and contradictions" are not "solved" per se. Rather, contradictions mark the complexity of human life, and the tension between the individual and the group characterizes the life experience of the dialectical thinker. Thus Coser sees *Lebensanschuung* as a failure for precisely the same reasons we may see it as a success: that it keeps open and alive the fundamental contradictions and tensions of human life and of Simmel's life as a theorist. Like Kuhn, Coser holds Simmel to the requirement of a reifiable solution—a paradigm—and fails to see Simmel's negation of the need for such a solution as the essential requirement of scientific activity.

Coser appreciates the "dialectic of social life" merely as a topic to be spoken about. Yet he cannot condone the dialectic's emergence in the character of Simmel's work. Thus Coser collapses the dialectic in order to keep it at a distance, as an abstract concept. He separates theory and practice and refuses to allow Simmel to live in the society that Simmel authored. Coser's criticism of Simmel's fragmented style, discussed earlier in this chapter, emerges as merely another example of this short-sightedness regarding the essence of the dialectic.

V

While fragmentation displays Simmel's manner of involvement with the contents of his writings, it cannot be formalized as method within a community of scientists. For Simmel, fragmentation becomes his stylistic manner in connection with, and as a consequence and symbol of, his experience of theorizing. Without this intimate link, fragmentation would lack any positive character and would rightly be subject to the criticisms leveled at Simmel. We can draw a partial comparison here with Franz Schubert's "Unfinished Symphony." The unfinishedness of the symphony becomes one of its analytic features inasmuch as the uniqueness of the piece unfolds partially through the unfinishedness. Yet unfinishedness cannot then become a formal method for composing further symphonies. That is, another composer could not reproduce the essence of Schubert's "Unfinished Symphony" simply by beginning to write a symphony and not finishing it. The core of Schubert's symphony is not determined by a particular structural method imposed beforehand. Rather, the character of unfinishedness emerges as a consequence of the symphony's composition.

For Simmel, his style as method cannot be divorced from his experience of theorizing. Instead, by virtue of his topical preoccupation with the theme of individuality, it produces a conception of method as a consequence of the individuality achieved in theorizing. For Simmel, any method imposed on a member by the scientific community binds that member and restricts his ability to articulate his individuality. Method imposed by the community is precisely what the individual must attempt to transcend, even as he is participating in the life of the group.[38] In contrast, an individual's method (his own style, structure, and foundation) must surface as a consequence and symbol of his experience of theorizing. In other words, for Simmel, method is the responsibility of individuals. Simmel does not supply others with method (other than encourage adventure which in itself is not method), nor does he attempt to perfect and consolidate a strong paradigm designed to subject other scientists (which is incidentally what Freud did once he first captured his individuality). There can be no paradigm for individuality. Remaining faithful to this theme, Simmel must attempt to live as a nonparadigmatic author. While a paradigm may be extracted from his writings (as von Wiese and Weingartner have done) and introduced into the scientific community as foundation and method, such a paradigm misses the deeper spirit of Simmel's authorship.

Simmel does not attempt to transform his struggle for individuality into a struggle for supremacy within the scientific community. In his concern for individuality he makes no attempt to violate the individuality of his audience. Through his writing Simmel can only become the exemplar of individuality within his scientific community. His commitment to the scientific community is not directed toward the concrete preservation of its paradigm, but to the individuals who as members of that community have not seen the possibility of a life of struggle for independence from the accepted community paradigm. In this sense Simmel's breaking through is not conceivable in terms of Kuhn's notion of a paradigm shift, or in terms of the solely concrete concern that he must have attracted a wide and unified following.[39] Rather, breakthrough, for Simmel, may be formulated in terms of his having provided a precedent and thus support for the achievement of individuality. In this sense, while his work will never be fully integrated within the scientific community's structure and ideology, it will greatly influence individuals within that community. Simmel has provoked many authors (Martin Buber, Robert Park, and Max Weber are only a few examples),[40] but they have not been restricted as a result of their relationship with him. His success is synonymous with his refusal to manage their procedure and direction. In one comment, Simmel formulates this notion as follows: "I know that I shall die without intellectual heirs, and that is as it should be. My legacy will be like cash, distributed to many heirs, each transforming his part into use according to his nature—a use which will no longer reveal its indebtedness to this heritage." [41]

4
BUBER

With Simmel we encountered an author who attempts not simply to break out of a particular paradigm, but out of paradigmatic work altogether. He displays how a paradigm structures our experience of theorizing by granting legitimacy to certain problems and certain methods for dealing with these problems, while ruling as illegitimate or uninteresting other directions of inquiry. Simmel's work testifies to the restrictions of paradigmatic work and represents an attempt to overcome them. The underlying theme of his corpus is the struggle for individuality. This theme, when pursued to its core, precludes the possibility of Simmel's offering a systematic paradigm to the scientific community.

Martin Buber has a similar relationship to paradigmatic work, although by virtue of a different concern. His trouble with paradigmatic work derives from a different characteristic of the notion of a "paradigm." The paradigm is a model, an objective representation of an achievement. Buber discovers, however, that certain achievements when preserved objectively lose virtually all of their intelligibility. The achievement of dialogue is the case in point. Buber's thoughts on dialogue represent an awareness of a realm of speaking (living) which always remains inaccessible to the objective attitude. For Buber, therefore, there can be no paradigm for dialogue. Thus like Simmel, his writings must constitute an attempt to show the inherent limits of paradigmatic work.

I

One striking feature of Buber's work is its simplicity. The Buber corpus is astoundingly large—a bibliography of well over five hundred items in different languages.[1] Yet throughout, the author's attention remains fixed upon one single, simple theme and his thought remains grounded in what seems to be a simple truth. This simplicity, however, can be deceptive and should not lead one to assume that Buber's thought can be easily formulated in a single sentence or a single paragraph, for when reproduced in a like manner, the outcome always proves unworthy of his achievement. Reduced to a simple, objective formulation, Buber's theme of dialogue loses virtually all of its substance.

Buber's audience seems to have experienced this same difficulty in their discussions of his work. They found that while his thoughts on dialogue had surfaced in his writings with an overwhelming simplicity, their meaning was still very difficult to grasp objectively. In other words, the simplest was not construed as the easiest. No one sentence or paragraph seemed to adequately capture the central spirit of the corpus. No single objective formulation contained and held to his audience's satisfaction the essence of his achievement. Thus from 1923, when I and Thou[2] was published (by its reputation and by Buber's own assessment, his central work), until his death in 1965, Buber was called upon again and again to clarify and rephrase the meaning of dialogue. He responded to this demand patiently and diligently in every one of his works and in most of his conversations.[3] Occasionally, he would approach his central theme from a different angle in order to facilitate seeing it anew. And he would often point to the same simple notions using different words or different imagery so that his audience would not be mystified by one powerful set of terms and become locked into a language before understanding what the language meant. Still, each formulation was inconclusive and Buber's audience kept asking for more. With all the elaborate, diligent, and patient clarification of the simple theme, it continued to evade objective formulation.

Buber's thinking would not become any easier to grasp objectively, however, if we were suddenly to suggest that his thinking is extremely complex and that its simplicity resides only on the surface. A book entitled The Philosophy of Martin Buber[4] appeared before Buber's death and contained articles by various authors discussing Buber's theory of knowledge, his philosophical anthropology, metaphysics, ethics, moral philosophy, political philosophy, philosophy of religion, philosophy of history, philosophy of existence, the relevance of his thought to the natural sciences, to psychotherapy, to education and aesthetics—all in all, a very complex reproduction and analysis of Buber's thought. Since the book had been prepared before his death, Buber was invited to respond to these papers, as befitting the philosophical tradition of dialogue. His response was especially interesting for in it Buber was forced to acknowledge just how often his commentators and analysts had misrepresented his thought.[5] While most of these authors had intended to represent Buber faithfully—to locate and perhaps then criticize the core of his philosophy—they often failed to do so throughout the volume. Buber's fifty-six-page response was organized almost totally around the consideration of these misrepresentations. It seems that the simple truth had often evaded the analysts.

This study will examine the evasive nature of Buber's thought, not for the purpose of finally overcoming this evasiveness, but to show that it must be understood as a necessary feature of his central theme. In other words, any effort to capture, contain, and preserve Buber's thought in an objective formulation constitutes a misrepresentation of Buber from the very beginning, a radical shift away from his ground. The objective formulation often neglects completely what Buber himself has to say about objective formulations. We may approach the Buber corpus with the intent to uncover his understanding of objective speech.

II

Buber often writes that the primal feature and goal of the human world is dialogue.[6] A human being facing the problem of his own fulfillment only does so as he orients himself to the movement from solitary to dialogical life.[7] Thus any situation in which a human being "really" addresses[8] another being (animate or inanimate)[9] or when he "really" responds to another's address, bears the mark of essential human life. Speech (language and gesture) arises out of this basic human feature. Says Buber, "Language never existed before address; . . . the world and destiny became language for . . . [humans] only in partnership." [10] Speech fulfills the primal nature of speech only during the occasion of authentic dialogue.[11]

However, says Buber, human speaking bears a curious characteristic: it often exists outside the occasion of dialogue.[12] That is, it need not constitute authentic address. Language and gesture in themselves make no specific demand that they be used only toward the fulfillment of their primal possibility. We are perfectly able to talk and write without really addressing anyone or anything. Thus while speech arose from the dialogical situation and resounds essentially from the human capacity and "passionate longing" [13] for dialogical life, it need not fulfill its own essential nature.

In a paper entitled "Dialogue," Buber discusses this two-fold feature of speech by recalling a personal experience during Easter, 1914.[14] He relates that during that Easter season, a number of men from various European countries (Buber was included) had gathered to establish an international body that would be prepared to intervene and perhaps dissolve the looming catastrophe which seemed fated for the peoples of Europe. During the meeting, a sense of urgency prevailed and led to the abandonment of formalities and social niceties usually characteristic of such international and interracial gatherings. In the course of their discussions, Buber and another participant became involved in a debate over the composition of this intended international body. Each strongly protested the other's views until, at one point, as a consequence of the intensity of the argument, both rose from their seats—presumably to continue their fight. However, when they stood facing each other, they stopped, embraced, and sat down. The argument had ended with the meeting of two penetrating glances.

Buber recalls this experience of the broken-off conversation in order to show how even the most well-intended argument, born out of an honest sense of urgency, can fail in its most essential category.[15] In their debate, the participants had failed to address each other. Buber would argue further that had the debate even proceeded to some concrete and objectively visible conclusion (as when one antagonist "wins" and the other "loses"), the speakers would have come no closer to fulfilling the nature of speech. This is precisely what the two speakers came to realize. With the breaking off of the conversation, both acknowledged that their argument had been conceived outside the dialogical situation. What had been lacking in the argument was the essence of speech itself.

Buber further suggests—and for him this is the most important aspect of the recollection—that with the breaking off of the argument speech was suddenly fulfilled.[16] On the surface, this suggestion might sound very arbitrary, for Buber does not at this point provide an objective, analytic rule whereby we could, with the same information, arrive at the same conclusion. That is, he formulates no objective criteria for the fulfillment of speech. He does not suggest, for example, that the speech was fulfilled by virtue of the silent glance that followed the argument. Nor does he wish us to believe that dialogue could somehow be contained within the fraternal embrace the speakers gave each other or even within the warm feeling it may have produced. While these are concrete features of this one particular dialogue and even essential to this concrete occasion, they are only contingent to dialogue itself. Just as language can be spoken in separation, so can a glance and an embrace be gestured and a warm feeling be experienced outside authentic address. The point that Buber wishes to make here is that authentic dialogue cannot be described. It cannot be demonstrated in any "objectively comprehensible form."[17] It does not surface within the "language of objects."[18]

Buber formulates this same notion in his article, "The Word That Is Spoken," when he writes, "if we could take an inventory of all the physical and psychic phenomena to be found within a dialogical event, there would still remain outside something sui generis that could not be included.... This something sui generis is their dialogue."[19] In this quote Buber wishes to emphasize the formal limitation of objective speech, but in a specific sense. Here, dialogue would be related to objective speech as the whole is related to the part. Buber makes this same suggestion in I and Thou when he writes, "But the language of objects catches only one corner of actual life."[20] However, for Buber, the distinction between objective speech and dialogue is significantly more deep-rooted than the simple relation between fraction and whole could suggest. In I and Thou, he refers to their distinction as a formal "opposition"[21] in the sense that both these manners of speaking resound from opposing ontological bases.

Dialogue resides in a situation of concrete, mutual relation between speakers. Its force emerges as this concreteness, as its exclusive presence within the moment of speech. Dialogue cannot outlive its moment or escape its participants without losing its force and transforming its nature. Thus it is only accessible to its participants and only to the extent that their relationship endures. In contrast, objective speech has no feeling for its moment, or whether during that moment its speakers enter into an authentic relation. Concern for the moment of speech and its bearing upon the essence of speech becomes suspended during the process of objectification. Objective speech must be accessible to anyone at any time. Thus, according to Buber, dialogue occupies an ontological ground "between" [22] its participants, while pure objectification escapes that ground.

III

Given this formal opposition of objective and dialogical speech and the standard by which each surfaces in human relations, we can see how Buber grounds his teaching of dialogue exclusively within the dialogical event. It is his contention that a full understanding[23] of dialogue can only emerge for the participants of the dialogical event and only for the event's duration. That is, dialogue can be seen only within dialogue.[24] But given this notion, Buber's writings themselves acquire a peculiar status. On the one hand, his writings are preserved outside the occasion of their having been spoken; they constitute objective speech. On the other hand, Buber's writings emphasize the formal limitation of objective speech. He must have realized, and must be attempting to impress upon his audience, that even his own writings are instances of the limitation he discusses. In other words, Buber would suggest that the essence of his thoughts on dialogue will evade even his own objective formulation of them. Consider his scattered references with regard to this theme. In "Replies to My Critics," he writes that he had to express in concepts "what is by nature incomprehensible in concepts." [25] Further on he writes, "These contents are not codifiable." [26] And in *I and Thou* the following sentences appear: "These moments are immortal; none are more evanescent. They leave no content that could be preserved." [27] Thus the writings themselves cannot contain and preserve the essence of what they write about.

But how does this differ from all writing? Is not all writing essentially incomplete? No description ever contains that which it purports to describe. It only becomes "the description" when it is negotiated as such, and only after decisions about the correspondence between the description and its concrete referent are made under commonsense auspices among the practical exigencies and relevance structure of the moment.[28] Thus how does the inexhaustible mystery of "dialogue" differ here from the inexhaustible mystery of a "sunshine" or a "toothache?" Does not the person with the toothache often shun our sympathy by saying the same thing I have just said about dialogue, that you can only see a toothache when you have one? Thus wherein lies the special status of dialogue that can distinguish it from other objects or phenomena within the concrete world—all indescribable—and permit the formulation of its unique evasiveness to objective speech?

The description of a toothache or a sunshine or a snail is indifferent to what it purports to describe until a correspondence is established in the social world. Then, for all practical purposes, this indifference is overcome and the description comes to represent its referent. Not so with dialogue. The objective description can never represent its referent. Dialogue evades its objective description in that it stands in opposition to the objective attitude. No practical exigencies can ever nullify this opposition. Here the description negates its referent and falsifies itself precisely at the moment when it claims to represent it.

IV

In "My Way to Hasidism," Buber writes that after delivering a lecture, he would often arrange to converse informally with a few members of his audience in order to re-enter the subject of his lecture in a situation more conducive to dialogue.[29] Here Buber emphasizes—as many other committed teachers have done—that dialogue with his audience is always concretely relevant within his capacity as a teacher. The lecture form, writes Buber, "allows no reply," therefore making it difficult to accomplish an authentic relation between speaker and audience. But clearly, the lecture itself does not preclude the possibility of such a relation. Buber would have to agree that on occasion, a lecture does surface as dialogue even though the response from the audience or from just one of its members may occur in silence[30] (for example, Buber's recollection of the broken-off conversation in which dialogue emerged outside language). Thus we may argue that Buber is not specifically concerned with the lecture per se when he mentions the problems and limits of lecturing, but with the lecture as a metaphor for objective speech and, in this case, speech-not-yet-engaged-or-no-longer-engaged-within-a-concrete-dialogical-situation. Moreover, if we recall Buber's notion of the limits of objective speech, especially with regard to the formulation of his own thought, we may further suggest that not only is dialogue concretely relevant for Buber, *it is also analytically relevant*. In other words, Buber's corpus, by itself, constitutes a limited achievement in the specific sense that it does not make itself fully intelligible *before it engages an audience*.

This notion of the analytic relevance of an audience finds suitable precedent for Buber in the Judaic tradition. Recall that the word of God as given to Moses had been preserved exclusively as an oral teaching transmitted from generation to generation by the tribal elders directly to the young. For many years this holy teaching was not written down, not given to objective speech. Thus a tradition developed which not only attempted to perpetuate the content of the teaching but to preserve the relationship through which the content retained its original force. The voice that speaks to human beings through the teaching was, for a long time, preserved as a living voice within a living relationship.

How much more powerful were the Ten Commandments, asks Buber, when pronounced within a living relationship, that is, when the "Thou" of the commandments referred specifically and exclusively to the one person being addressed? And how much less of an address to the human soul was this decalogue when it surfaced as an impersonal system of laws? [31] At the moment in Judaic history when the teaching emerged within the frame of the written Bible, such a relation was lost and the fuller impact of the teaching was lost as well. Of course, Buber says that it can always be retrieved by a reader who reads in such a way that the Bible begins to speak to him personally. But before such a reading the Bible cannot yet surface with its original force.[32]

This reference to the Bible as speech-not-yet-engaged-in-a-dialogical-relation, and Buber's similar reference to the lecture as speech-not-yet-engaged, point to a particular characteristic of objective speech—the notion that objective speech can be understood in terms of its underlying unfinishedness. Consider the meaning of "finishing" from its etymological source. The word originally comes from the Latin "finis" which not only means to end or to complete, but also to reach the highest point, the summit. Current English usage has dropped this latter aspect of the primordial grammar; the term no longer makes reference to the higher possibilities of the project under way, that is, to a standard that a project must achieve. All this is regarded as a matter of personal decision and subject to practical issues such as time and available resources, or to psychological issues such as motivation. In the original Latin, however, the notion of finishing expressed a profound commitment to the project under way inasmuch as no undertaking could truly be finished before it realized its highest goal.

Buber embraces this notion of "finishing" in its etymological sense. He is concerned with the essential unfinishedness of objective speech especially with regard to a proper understanding of his own thought. He refuses to acknowledge the corpus itself as the authoritative recipient of the highest standard of speech. While Buber may complete a written work in the sense of submitting it for publication as a self-contained piece with beginning chapter, middle chapters, and a closing one, he will still not credit the work with the attribute of authentic finishedness. More important, it is not within the realm of his capabilities to finish the work by himself. The solitary voice can only create the sound of the unfinished, unfulfilled soul. Only a reader can render the work dialogical. Only another can perform the task of finishing, and then only with reference to one concrete moment and one concrete relation. Once this moment passes, unfinishedness reappears.

Who is the reader on whom Buber places this responsibility of finishing the work? How can we begin to hear the resonances of his task, his character, and his responsibility? Buber formulates the reader in terms of his "readiness." [33] Readiness, as Buber uses it, must be understood both in an active and passive sense.[34] In its passive sense, readiness for dialogue implies waiting, as when we are fully prepared for something to happen that we cannot control. When we are ready it means that there is nothing more for us to prepare, no activity left for us to consider. The prepared soldier before the attack, the prepared entertainer before the performance, the prepared bride before the ceremony, have only to wait. Waiting however, can produce a certain tension, and because of this tension readiness must assume its active nature. Here readiness implies not only that we wait, but that we wait firmly, in the face of a deep temptation to wait no longer, to flee and seek more available and tangible rewards for which we need not wait. But dialogue is not tangible, nor is it readily available. It occurs only amidst the activity and passivity of readiness, in the coming together of "will and grace," [35] necessity and chance.

Buber speaks of three kinds of readers: the "amicus" reads the work and knows what it points to; the "adversarius" reads the work and denies what it points to; and the "inimicus" reads the work, finds there a system of ideas, and carries its subject away from the concrete world into the world of ideology. Buber writes that he would hope for the first two readers, but would "gladly dispense" with the third.[36]

What distinguishes "amicus" and "adversarius" from "inimicus" is that the latter sees no virtue in waiting. He must always quickly extract concrete ideas and interpretations from his reading. For him, reading has no positive value without these tangible rewards. He cannot see reading itself (the participation itself) as a reward. "Inimicus" shuns any real encounter with Other, for he feels he must always be in control. Who is Other but someone we cannot control,[37] someone for whom we must wait, someone who may not come at all? Waiting constitutes a reliance on the uncontrollable—on grace. Thus for "inimicus," grace possesses only a negative character which he tries to push out of his teleological system. He will count on nothing outside of what he himself can dominate and manipulate. He does not rely on Other when he writes; he refuses to be Other when he reads. "Inimicus" defends himself against grace; he may not even see it when it comes.

Waiting therefore implies an inability to affirm the ownership of a subject. "Inimicus" differs from "amicus" and "adversarius" in this sense: he presents his speech (and his response) as the authoritative recipient of a subject. He allows for a speedy beginning by eliminating the necessity of waiting; he treats waiting as an unnecessary delay—even as cowardice. The authority of this attitude lies in the optimism it generates by being able to begin alone. Other is invited into the speech, but only to the extent that Other's hearing and speaking fit the frame created within and by the solitary beginning. The real Otherness of the Other—which cannot be contained within the limits of that beginning, and for which we must wait—is converted into an object of hatred.

Thus for "inimicus," being ready has no positive status of its own. He will always ask "Ready for what?" and will find meaning in readiness only in terms of some pre-established content for which he is ready. But contrast him with the other two readers, whom Buber prefers: while "amicus" and "adversarius" are opposites in many respects, they are alike in their readiness. Both are comparable in terms of their will to wait—"amicus" for the encounter, and "adversarius" for the fight that may become an encounter. Both are ready to face an Other who is unknown and uncontrollable.

V

While the notion of unfinishedness has been used here to refer to the formal limits of objective speech, for Buber it does not necessarily mean the failure of objective speech. To be sure, Buber does not often celebrate the language of objects—in fact, he has intimated that it has already been sufficiently celebrated.[38] But neither does he wish it destroyed. The objective attitude has the unique capacity to preserve speech and to allow it to reach a wider audience; Buber, both as a member of the audience of other authors and as a speaker to a wide, unnamed audience, is thankful for this capacity. In other words, he does not choose to avoid speaking altogether merely because his speech may be spoken outside authentic address. In *I and Thou*, for example, he writes that the language of objects can "serve the truth" by "defining the limit every day anew, according to the right and measure of that day."[39]

Objective speech does not fail because it has limits. Rather, it fails when it disavows its limits and thus obstructs the direction to authentic dialogue. It fails when it renounces its higher possibilities in order to establish its own authority and control over a subject. For Buber, to be not-yet-finished means to be facing one's immediate limits and thus to be turned (re-turned) in the direction of one's dialogical possibilities.[40]

If the beginning of the dialogical commitment resides in its aim toward an authentic finishedness, then the solitary beginning must know that it has not yet begun in its essence. To forget this is to allow speech to mask the crisis of its origin—as beginning before it has really begun. Hence, the dialogical commitment must mean that the speaker hears his speech in terms of the crisis of beginning prematurely. Other is always the sole threat to the finishedness implied in or aimed for in the beginning. Whatever secure constitution of self, whatever self-system is produced in the beginning, "it melts away before the steady gaze of another."[41] To wait for Other's gaze is to resist the authority of the premature beginning.

I have suggested that Buber's work introduces a certain problem for readers in that it evades the reader's grasp. But this evasiveness in and by itself does not determine the full extent of the problem. The problem results partly from our having given evasiveness a negative valuation. Within our intellectual community we call on others' achievements to formally guide our work. Kuhn, as we recall, calls these achievements "paradigmatic" in that they mark off a secure position (and direction) and set themselves as models for further research.[42] An evasive achievement cannot function adequately as a Kuhnian "paradigm," for it cannot formally and concretely direct intellectual work.

Traditionally, a paradigm is not questioned, nor does it question itself, for its ability to be formulated objectively. Usually some formulation or even various formulations (either in the original corpus or in textbooks on the subject) are recognized within the respective intellectual community as adequate and complete (finished) representations of the paradigm. And since the objective formulation can be preserved, the paradigm it represents will give itself to anyone who picks it up. It is understood and accepted that one need only master the formulation (the formula) to master the paradigm (the achievement). He need not achieve it himself, but only passively accept its authority. With Buber's corpus, however, disregarding the distinction between the achievement of dialogue and an objective formulation of this achievement would result in a misapprehension of Buber's thinking, for it would dissolve his central distinction between dialogical and objective speech. For Buber, then, one can know the formula without achieving dialogue.[43] Dialogue evades that reader who expects to discover a completed formula within the pages of the corpus.

"I have no teaching," writes Buber.[44] Here he renounces all authority that his writings may acquire as paradigmatic work within his intellectual community. Buber has "no teaching" inasmuch as his corpus cannot own dialogue. Dialogue may be grasped during its moment, but then it withdraws from its owner at the very instant he would wish to reflect upon it and formulate it. The corpus only "points" outside of itself to that which must remain outside of itself.[45]

In the act of pointing, Buber's speech bears the ontological contradiction of speaking about dialogue alone. By pointing outside of itself, the speech occupies a position while its own subject withdraws. But by pointing, Buber resists the authoritative character of that position he holds, and warns his reader not to read from within the objective position of the speech, but in the direction in which it points.

Paradigmatic work would have a reader read otherwise. The paradigm holds people together by keeping them in one position. A paradigm for dialogue (certainly a contradiction in terms) would think of its own objectively formulated position as the place where

both One and Other ought to be,[46] and would have dialogue meet
the limiting requirement of its secured position. But in the very act
of affirming the position as representing dialogue, it rules out the
possibility of dialogue. Thus, pointing makes reference to a concrete
obstacle which stands in the way of Buber's thought, and it represents Buber's departure from the conventional standard of addressing
speech held within his intellectual community.

But for Buber, dialogue does not merely constitute a peripheral
topic—an incidental adjunct—that cannot be contained objectively.
The dialogical commitment pursued in accordance with its nature re-
centers all speech and relates it back to its primal motives in human
relationship. The intellectual community's failure to sustain the meaning of dialogue represents not only a shift away from a single topic,
but away from the capacity of humans to communicate. Buber uses
the term "alien place" [47] to refer to social structures which have emp-
tied themselves of their relational content. Human beings, he writes,
are "in a growing measure . . . [objectively] determined." [48] This constitutes a severe obstacle to the deeper possibilities residing in speech.
Buber formulates his audience in the face of this dilemma and with
them, will make no attempt to strengthen objective analysis. He produces no paradigm, no objectively conclusive system of thought. Rather,
he points to the formal limits of objective analysis; he tries to speak to
people rather than to a paradigm. On the rare occasions that he does
address a particular paradigm, he does so only to dissolve its authority
over human speech and its interference with human relationships.

VI

Various analysts of Buber's work have observed that when Buber discusses the realm of dialogue, he approaches it negatively by renounc-
ing what it is not, before pointing to what it is.[49] For this reason his
thinking has been labeled "negative ontology." [50] The negation of an
ontology, however, speaks to Buber's experience of theorizing, and represents the writer's route, aimed at overturning a standard of reading
entrenched within the intellectual community. The only way Buber
can enter into the realm of objective speech and remain faithful to the
subject of his work, is by focusing on the inherent limits of objective
speech. Our intellectual community traditionally organizes work with
the same attitude toward objective speech as does Kuhn in his discus-

sions of the necessity of a paradigm.[51] We invest significant writings with an authority that Buber does not want; to give his writings this authority would only result in a misapprehension of the meaning of his thought. Buber recognizes this obstacle and attempts to convert the conventional relationship to the objective attitude. To this end, he not only enunciates but also grounds his work in the distinction between objective and dialogical speech, in order to display that his corpus does not contain a model and thus cannot be read as if no further achievement is required. To explain his work within a tradition that would rule against its being understood, Buber must violate the authority of objective speech and dissolve the notion of the uninvolved reader before he could ever really engage a reader and make him responsible for the achievement of dialogue.

5
SUMMARY

I   As a topic of sociological inquiry, intellectual breakthrough refers to a number of related social phenomena:
the tendency of an intellectual community to restrict the individuality
of its members; the struggle of certain members against restrictions imposed upon them; and the overcoming of some of these restrictions by
developing a new idea, a new style, a new paradigm, a new teaching.
These studies investigated the topic empirically, examining the works
of Sigmund Freud, Georg Simmel, and Martin Buber in an attempt
to show how these authors' ideas related to the restrictive situations
through which they emerged.

The chapter on Freud noted that psychoanalytic theory focuses most
specifically upon the essential tension between the individual and the
group. I argued that Freud's discussion of this tension can be interpreted as a metaphoric representation of his own inimical relationship
to the scientific community. Seen in this way, we can expose certain
contradictory impulses characteristic of Freud's experience of theorizing. On the one hand, Freud was committed to preserving science as a
major source of practical (and in this case, medical) wisdom. On the
other hand, his own investigations show how the rule of unequivocal
speech—a rule upon which the structure of science rests—was secured
by repressing human desires. I argued that the notion of "the symbol"
enables Freud to avoid having to collapse this contradiction. In fact,
the notion of the symbol retains and embodies this same contradiction.

The symbol possesses a dual life: a concrete life adhering to the limits of unequivocal speech, and a hidden life responding to the plurivocal capacity of speech and from which the suppressed and muted voice of Desire speaks. Thus with the symbol as the nexus of Freud's contradictory impulses, his corpus can preserve science as the pursuit of practical wisdom while simultaneously exposing the violence it does to human expression.

The chapter on Simmel noted the fragmentary character of the author's corpus and his principled reluctance to unify the work into a systematic whole. I observed how this characteristic of Simmel's writings led to severe criticism by members of the scientific community. However, rather than criticize this characteristic myself, I showed how this fragmentary style may be considered an essential feature of the Simmelian project. In his article "The Adventure," Simmel suggests one positive feature of fragmentation: the commitment to meet every situation directly without the imposition of an alien structure and method—a structure imposed upon a topic of inquiry before the inquiry begins. Here Simmel alludes to the restrictive capacities of systematic unity in writing. I suggested that given this notion, the fragmentary character of his writing constitutes a style of opposition to certain restrictions imposed upon inquiry from outside. I further suggested that it expresses Simmel's commitment to the achievement of individuality: he neither imposes a strict, pre-established structure upon his own inquiry, nor unifies his writings with the intent of imposing a structure upon his audience.

The chapter on Buber began by noting that, due to the nature of dialogue, Buber's thought tends to evade any objective formulation. Dialogue lives only during the dialogical event and only between its participants. While we may extract a meaning from a particular dialogical event and preserve it as objective speech, we will not have retained its dialogical character. I suggested that since Buber himself realized this formal limitation of objective speech, he cannot present his corpus as the authoritative explanation of his own theme of dialogue. This in itself constitutes a radical departure from the experience prevalent within an intellectual community that is mostly confident in its capacity to formulate any teaching objectively. Buber's work struggles to overcome this achieved sense of confidence. His writings can only point to a dimension of speech—a human dimension—which cannot be contained within the attitude of objectivity.

II

My concern is a common one: How can we account for intellectual breakthrough? I attempted to find within that topic its necessity, that which called out to be addressed. In my discussions of Freud, Simmel, and Buber I showed how each author, in his work, had to challenge institutionally situated conventions that would limit the possibilities of his inquiry. Underlying the particular topics that each author dealt with, then, was a relation to the intellectual community made problematic by his own work. Yet this problem underlies all inquiry. My choice of addressing the phenomenon of intellectual breakthrough was an attempt to consider questions wider than breakthrough itself.

The pivotal theme of these studies has been the relation between the author and his intellectual community. The ancient Greeks held to the motto "know thyself." This same culture that witnessed the beginnings of Western philosophy and science, and the beginnings of a generative community of inquirers, always reminded its adherents to sustain a memory of the omnipresent tension between themselves and the community that supported them.

The philosophical notion of discourse (as dis-course) retains that memory throughout the history of Western philosophy. But while the intellectual community, as the official carrier of Western philosophy, speaks the language of discourse, it tends to devalue its source in the context of collective inquiry. Given the organizational commitment to the expansion of knowledge, the intellectual community instructs its members to disregard the essential tension between the individual and the group. Thomas Kuhn attempts to recover this tension by reporting the struggles accompanying scientific revolutions. But as I noted earlier, Kuhn defines his topic in terms of what the postrevolutionary community is willing to embrace within its new boundaries—as if this community, recognized for its long periods of slumber, is ever fully awakened to the discursive content of its monumental works. The new community bears the essential characteristics of the old: in its commitment to expand knowledge, it limits inquiry to the world defined by its paradigm. Thus a history of discourse is not the same as a history of paradigm shifts within the intellectual community.

In order to remind ourselves of the essential tensions between the individual and the group, we must ask what portion of ourselves have we locked away, and continue to lock away, in the course of this institutionalized and systematic surge toward knowledge? With Freud we see a scientific community that narrows the possibilities of language and, as such, hides the richness that language possesses. With Simmel we see a scientific community that imposes an alien structure and method upon human inquiry, thereby severely limiting the inquirer's possibilities. With Buber we see a philosophical community that cannot recognize the limits of objective speech and, as such, fails to realize the essential purpose of speech.

These studies have attempted to show how the intellectual community adopts a particular orientation to intellectual work (a paradigm) while expecting its members to represent the same orientation mimetically. Intellectual institutions (like the university) in our society that claim to understand and speak for Western intellectual tradition, have often lost the very spirit of that tradition because of their self-limiting orientations. Their structuring of thought has made it inconsistent with thinking itself. Members of these institutions, who have submitted to institutional rule, have become merely its instruments. But more, they have violated the tradition from which they pretend to speak. The monumental moments of that tradition were certainly not moments of mimesis. They were ones of reflection, critique, and discourse. As critical thinkers Freud, Simmel, and Buber represent the heart of that tradition.

Authors of breakthrough are often discussed merely as "model members" of the intellectual community—as "contributors" to a body of knowledge and to a culture we now own: Darwin contributed the theory of evolution; Newton contributed the laws of motion; Freud contributed the psychoanalytic method. But these authors were not simply model members and contributors. They were thinkers who questioned and criticized the intellectual communities in which they participated. Too often we forget that aspect of their struggle. And even when we recognize the discursive spirit of their work, we often regard it as a critique of a particular intellectual community and orientation long passed into oblivion. We consider ourselves more educated, and believe that certainly these authors would not be critical of us and our contemporary intellectual community. But although we can find these authors' works displayed in our drugstores,[1] let us not assume that we have integrated the essence of their work into our "high culture" as we have done with fine wine or delicate jewelry. Herbert Marcuse warns us in *One-Dimensional Man* not to conceive of these individuals merely as "classics" (as members of the highest *class*), for "coming to life as classics, they come to life as other than themselves; they are deprived of their antagonistic force, of the estrangement which was the very dimension of their truth."[2]

For Freud, Simmel, and Buber, breakthrough begins with this estrangement—this relatedness to the tension between the individual and the group. But they express this estrangement in a certain way; not by escaping or declaring indifference, but by attempting to generate more relevant and crucial possibilities for inquiry. They choose to struggle with the restrictive conditions of their membership in an attempt to renegotiate conditions suitable to their own experiences of theorizing. And in order to amend or dissolve the accepted paradigm, they articulate their critiques and provide a higher rationality—one that allows their work to reach an audience and to re-enter the community of discourse.

NOTES

Chapter 1

1. From Hegel's preface to *The Phenomenology of Mind*, in *Hegel: Texts and Commentary*, ed. and trans. Walter Kaufmann (Garden City, N.Y.: Anchor Books, 1966), p. 10.

2. The term "analytic" appears throughout the book, and refers to that which is inherent to, or implied in, a subject. In contrast, the "concrete" refers to that which is connected with the subject only because the two happen to occur together in the phenomenon being examined, not because of any inherent or necessary connection between them.

3. See Ludwig Wittgenstein, *Philosophical Investigations*, trans. G. E. M. Anscombe (Oxford: Basil Blackwell, 1968), nos. 19, 23, 241.

4. See Michael Polanyi, *The Tacit Dimension* (Garden City, N.Y.: Anchor Books, 1966).

5. In *The Sociology of Georg Simmel*, ed. and trans. Kurt H. Wolff (New York: The Free Press, 1950), pp. 402–8.

6. "Human Migration and the Marginal Man," in Park, *Race and Culture* (New York: The Free Press, 1950), pp. 345–56.

7. *The Marginal Man* (New York: Scribner, 1937).

8. "The Stranger," in Schutz, *Collected Papers II*, ed. Arvid Brodersen (The Hague: Martinus Nijhoff, 1964), pp. 91–105.

9. Wolff, *Sociology of Georg Simmel*, p. 402.

10. Ibid., pp. 404–5.

11. Thorstein Veblen, "The Intellectual Pre-eminence of Jews in Modern Europe," in *The Portable Veblen*, ed. Max Lerner (New York: Viking Press, 1948), pp. 467–79.

12. The convert confuses his concrete and analytic grounds; that is, he

forgets the analytic and thinks of the tension it provided as a function
of his concrete troubles. Hence he becomes pure(ly) convention. Con-
version is thus a kind of erotic collapse of difference into concrete
identity.

13. In the study on Freud, I again take up the issue of the adequacy of
this form of explanation.

14. (Chicago: The University of Chicago Press, 1970).

15. In chapter 13 and in the postscript of *The Structure of Scientific
Revolutions,* and in "Reflections on My Critics," in *Criticism and the
Growth of Knowledge,* ed. Imre Lakatos and Alan Musgrave (Cambridge: Cambridge University Press, 1970), pp. 231–78, Kuhn argues
that while certain of his insights refer to processes evidenced in a
community wider than the scientific, other equally relevant categories
that he locates are features of science alone: (1) the fact that in science, novelty for its own sake is of no value; (2) that in science, the
unit of achievement is the solved problem; (3) that the mature sciences witness a relative scarcity of competing paradigms; (4) that in
the scientific community members work primarily for an audience of
colleagues; (5) that in the education of scientists textbooks are used
instead of the paradigmatic literature on which they rely. While we
could address the adequacy of these demarcations between science and
nonscience, my discussion will rely neither on their adequacy nor in-
adequacy. A reader who is interested may consult Karl Popper, "Normal Science and its Dangers," or Paul Feyerabend, "Consolations for
the Specialist," both in Lakatos and Musgrave, *Knowledge,* pp. 51–
58 and 197–230, respectively.

16. This notion is not negated by the well-known fact that for political
reasons, certain scientists keep their work from the public domain (the
wider scientific community). In this case, secret knowledge produces
secret communities smaller in size than the wider community and organized by the State rather than according to a given scientific problematic.

17. Kuhn, *Scientific Revolutions,* p. 23.

18. Ibid., pp. 52–53.

19. Ibid., p. 89.

20. Ibid., p. 79.

21. Kuhn briefly develops another feature of scientific breakthrough that
refers to its historical nature as an inquiry into grounds. He produces
evidence to suggest that scientists fight vehemently to protect the
paradigm under which they practice when they find it threatened
(Ibid., p. 64). What Kuhn says about this resistance by scientists to
departures from the paradigm is that it has a distinctly positive value
for scientific breakthrough and for the inquirer, in his challenge to the

community. Says Kuhn, the stronger the negative reaction from the community, the deeper inquiry must go in order to articulate its critique (Ibid., p. 65). In other words, the community's wish to preserve its orientation requires that the inquirer arrive at the deeper levels of the foundation of the paradigm in order to produce an adequate critique. Thus according to Kuhn, the more intense the struggle, the higher the dividends. Note the Darwinian conception of intellectual history implied in this statement: scientific breakthrough as the survival of the fittest enquirer. In his paper on Kuhn (Lakatos and Musgrave, *Knowledge*, p. 55), Popper reiterates this. "The dogmatic scientist has an important role to play," argues Popper. "If he gives in to criticism too easily, we shall never find out where the real power of our theories lies."

22. Lakatos and Musgrave, *Knowledge*, p. 79. Kuhn would argue here that this statement about the necessity of paradigms applies only to the mature sciences. But then he proceeds to define "mature science" as those sciences which operate under a paradigm. He makes no attempt to break the circularity of this definition in order to address the grounds of its intelligibility as an analytic feature of science and therefore its distinguishability from processes in the wider intellectual community.

23. The reader will note that Kuhn does not use the term "breakthrough" in his discussion; rather, he uses the term "revolution." However, for Kuhn, the phenomenon of scientific revolution includes versions of both breakthrough and revolution. Kuhn sees no reason to separate the two. Earlier in this discussion I explained my reasons for making such a separation: that each of these phenomena orient to a different complex of processes and commitments, one which I wished to study and the other which I did not.

24. Kuhn, *Scientific Revolutions*, pp. 52–53.

25. Ibid., p. 67.

26. Ibid., p. 93 ff.

27. Ibid., p. 89.

28. See Vico's formulation of "Topics" in *The New Science of Giambattista Vico*, rev. trans. T. G. Bergin and M. H. Fisch (Ithaca: Cornell University Press, 1968), no. 497. See also Ernesto Grassi, "Critical or Topical Philosophy? Meditations on the De nostri temperis studiorum ratione," trans. Hayden V. White, in Giorgio Tagliacozzo, ed., *Giambattista Vico, An International Symposium* (Baltimore: Johns Hopkins Press, 1969), pp. 39–50.

29. See the first pages of *What Is Philosophy?*, trans. Jean T. Wilde and William Kluback (New Haven, Conn.: College and University Press, 1956), where Heidegger addresses this question of how to proceed

without first having a secured and bounded topic. See also his *Intro-duction to Metaphysics*, trans. Ralph Manheim (Garden City, N.Y.: Anchor Books, 1961), pp. 10–11, where he refers to philosophy as "an extra-ordinary inquiry into the extra-ordinary."

Chapter 2

1. Ernest Jones, *Sigmund Freud: Life and Work* (London: Hogarth Press, 1953), vol. 1, preface.
2. Ibid., p. 2.
3. Ibid., p. 12.
4. From Hegel's preface to *The Phenomenology of Mind*, in *Hegel: Texts and Commentary*, ed. and trans. Walter Kaufmann (Garden City, N.Y.: Anchor Books, 1966), p. 10.
5. Henri F. Ellenberger, *The Discovery of the Unconscious* (New York: Basic Books, 1970). Ellenberger mentions the theme, however, only to dispute its objective relevance.
6. I have drawn from *The Origins of Psycho-Analysis: Letters to Wilhelm Fliess*, ed. Ernst Kris, Marie Bonaparte and Anna Freud, trans. Eric Mosbacher and James Strachey (New York: Basic Books, 1954).
7. This and all further references to Freud's psychological writings will be taken from *The Standard Edition of the Complete Psychological Works of Sigmund Freud* (hereafter cited as S.E.), 24 vols. (London: Hogarth Press and the Institute of Psycho-Analysis, 1953–1974); Freud, *An Autobiographical Study* (1925), S.E. 20; Freud, *On the History of the Psycho-Analytic Movement* (1914), S.E. 14.
8. Ellenberger, *Unconscious*, p. 435; Jones, *Freud*, vol. 1, pp. 372–74; Kris, *Fliess*, letters 151 and 152, pp. 341–44.
9. Freud, "The Aetiology of Hysteria" (1896), S.E. 3, pp. 189–221.
10. Jones, *Freud*, vol. 1, pp. 289–90.
11. Joseph Breuer and Sigmund Freud, *Studies in Hysteria* (1893–95), S.E. 2.
12. See the footnote to letter 40 in Kris, *Fliess*, p. 156.
13. Freud, "Preface to Reik's *Ritual: Psycho-Analytic Studies*" (1919), S.E. 17, p. 259.
14. Freud, "On Beginning the Treatment" (1913), S.E. 12, pp. 134–35.
15. It may be asked here why I have not formulated a distinction between ordinary conversation and neurotic talk. I have made no such distinc-tion, not because it could not be formulated but because, in the con-text of this discussion, the distinction would be insignificant. Within the framework of psychoanalysis, neurotic talk and ordinary conversa-tion are the same methodologically and in the context of this discus-sion, it is the method that is of primary concern. Freud bases his

discussion in *The Psychopathology of Everyday Life* (1901), S.E. 6, on this same notion.

16. Later we will see how authentic speech takes on a double meaning in the work of psychoanalysis. The first responds to the lifting of restrictions imposed by the community and the second responds to the placing of restrictions on members for practical reasons.

17. For an excellent discussion of the status of the scientific superstructure and its power over ordinary life, read Trent Shroyer, "Toward a Critical Theory for Advanced Industrial Society," in Hans P. Dreitzel, *Recent Sociology no. 2* (New York: The MacMillan Company, 1970), pp. 210–34.

18. Freud, "Fragment of an Analysis of a Case of Hysteria" (1905), S.E. 7, pp. 9, 48–51.

19. Kris, *Fliess*, letters 18, 41, 43, 50, 126, 127, 142.

20. Ibid., letter 142.

21. Freud brings up this issue much less candidly in *An Autobiographical Study* (1925), S.E. 20. It is interesting that even as late as 1924 when his work had already won its respectability within the scientific community Freud's animosity toward these events of his early career did not disappear. His references to his early years were still marked with a severe bitterness for the scientific community that did not respond favorably to his early work. He speaks about the "arrogance," "coarseness," "contempt of logic," and "bad taste" of his colleagues (p. 49). He sarcastically refers to the scientific community's "official anathema against psychoanalysis" (p. 50). "When the history of the phase we have lived through comes to be written," writes Freud, "German science will not have cause to be proud of those who represented it." (p. 49).

22. Freud, *On the History of the Psycho-Analytic Movement* (1914), S.E. 14, p. 16.

23. Freud, "Repression," (1915), S.E. 14, p. 147.

24. See Georg Simmel's discussion of sociability in *The Sociology of Georg Simmel*, ed. and trans. Kurt H. Wolff (New York: The Free Press, 1950), pp. 40–57.

25. The term is Freud's. See *The Interpretation of Dreams* (1900), S.E. 5, p. 548.

26. See Søren Kierkegaard, "The Sickness unto Death" in *Fear and Trembling and the Sickness unto Death*, trans. Walter Lowrie (Princeton, N.J.: Princeton University Press, 1941).

27. Martin Heidegger, *What Is Called Thinking?*, trans. Fred D. Wieck and J. Glenn Gray (New York: Harper and Row, 1968), p. 11.

28. Freud, "Screen Memories" (1899), S.E. 3, pp. 301–22.

29. Ibid., p. 306.

30. Ibid., p. 306.
31. Freud, *The Future of an Illusion* (1927), S.E. 21.
32. Freud, *Totem and Taboo* (1913), S.E. 13.
33. Locating hidden memory within speech is, of course, the central focus of psychoanalytic procedure.
34. Nietzsche uses "understand" as "standing under." Read the "under" and "over" imagery in the prologue of *Thus Spoke Zarathustra*, in *The Portable Nietzsche*, trans. and ed. Walter Kaufmann (New York: The Viking Press, 1954), pp. 121–37.
35. Read Alan Blum's discussion of truth as "faithfulness," in *Theorizing* (London: Heinemann, 1974), chap. 3.
36. Ibid.
37. Ibid.
38. Freud, "From the History of an Infantile Neurosis" (1918), S.E. 17, pp. 3–122.
39. Ibid. See also *Introductory Lectures on Psycho-Analysis* (1916–17), S.E. 16, p. 371.
40. Freud, *Totem and Taboo* (1913), S.E. 13, pp. 141–46. See also chap. 10, "The Group and the Primal Horde," in *Group Psychology and the Analysis of the Ego* (1921), S.E. 18, pp. 122–28.
41. Freud, "Repression" (1915), S.E. 14, p. 148.
42. Freud, "The Taboo of Virginity" (1918), S.E. 11, pp. 197–98.
43. Freud, lecture 22 of *Introductory Lectures on Psycho-Analysis* (1916–17), S.E. 16, pp. 340–42.
44. Ibid., lecture 23, pp. 364–65.
45. With this distinction we may see the difference between Freud and Otto Rank. Rank's assertion was that concrete birth is always the primal scene, and, as such, the analytic beginning. See Rank, *The Myth of the Birth of the Hero*, ed. Phillip Freund, trans. F. Robbins and Smith Ely Jelliffe (New York: Vintage Books, 1932).
46. My reference to "fixation" as "beginning" and "end" relies upon Freud's similar usage of the term. He refers to fixation as the attachment of an instinct to an object which marks both a beginning of a symptom and an end in the development of the instinct. See editor's note 1 in "A Case of Successful Treatment of Hypnotism" (1892–93), S.E. 1, p. 125.
47. Blum, *Theorizing*, chap. 1.
48. Aristotle, *Metaphysics*, A1 982 a 20, A1 981 a 25, A1 981 b 8, in *The Basic Works of Aristotle*, ed. Richard McKeon (New York: Random House, 1941), pp. 689–91.
49. Ibid., A1 982 a 27, p. 691.
50. Ibid., A1 980 α 21, A2 982 b 12, pp. 639 and 692, respectively.
51. Read the *Symposium*, for example.

52. Stanley Rosen, "Σωφροσύνη and Selbstbewusstsein," *Review of Metaphysics*, vol. 26, no. 4, June 1973.
53. Freud discusses the development of the reality principle in "Formulations on the Two Principles of Mental Functioning" (1911), *S.E.* 12, pp. 213–26.
54. In the preface to the third English edition of *The Interpretation of Dreams*, Freud writes that the book "contains . . . the most valuable of the discoveries it has been my good fortune to make." *S.E.* 4, p. xxxii.
55. Aristotle, *Metaphysics*, 1006 b 7, p. 738.
56. Nietzsche, *Zarathustra*, p. 130.
57. This argument is developed in Blum, *Theorizing*, chap. 3.
58. Paul Ricoeur, *Freud and Philosophy*, trans. Denis Savage (New Haven: Yale University Press, 1970), p. 38.
59. Freud, "Delusions and Dreams in Jensen's Gradiva" (1907), *S.E.* 9; "Creative Writers and Day-Dreaming" (1908), *S.E.* 9; "The Theme of the Three Caskets" (1913), *S.E.* 12; "Dostoevsky and Parricide" (1928), *S.E.* 21.
60. Freud, "The Moses of Michelangelo" (1914), *S.E.* 13.
61. Freud, *Civilization and Its Discontents* (1930), *S.E.* 21; "Why War?" (1933), *S.E.* 22.
62. Freud, "Psycho-Analysis and the Establishment of the Facts in Legal Proceedings" (1906), *S.E.* 9.
63. Freud, "Obsessive Actions and Religious Practices" (1907), *S.E.* 9; *The Future of an Illusion* (1927), *S.E.* 21; "A Religious Experience" (1928), *S.E.* 21.
64. Freud, *The Future of an Illusion* (1927), *S.E.* 21.
65. See footnote 61, above.

Chapter 3

1. See Emile Durkheim, "Sociology and Its Scientific Field," ed. and trans. Kurt H. Wolff, in *Emile Durkheim, 1858–1917* (Columbus, Ohio: Ohio State University Press, 1960), pp. 354–75.
2. Ibid., p. 359.
3. Pitirim Sorokin, "A Critique of Simmel's Method," in Lewis Coser, ed., *Georg Simmel* (Englewood Cliffs, N.J.: Prentice-Hall, 1965), p. 148.
4. Reproduced in Donald Levine's introduction to Georg Simmel, *On Individuality and Social Forms*, ed. Donald N. Levine (Chicago: University of Chicago Press, 1971), p. xlvi.
5. Ibid., p. xlvi. The above comments of Weber were taken from a critique of Simmel's work which Weber began to write but never

finished. It seems that at the time, Simmel was being considered for an academic position and Weber did not want to hurt his chances. Levine refers to this on p. xlv.

6. Leopold von Wiese, "Simmel's Formal Method," trans. Martin Nicolaus, in Coser, *Simmel*, p. 56.

7. Rudolph Weingartner would disagree with the above statement. In his *Experience and Culture: The Philosophy of Georg Simmel* (Middletown, Conn.: Wesleyan University Press, 1960), he does claim to see more system in Simmel than the other critics have seen.

8. Let me anticipate a certain criticism. It may be argued that Simmel is not the proper author through which to address the topic of systematic unity in science, for Simmel is not really a scientist. This, however, would contradict his own statements on the subject. See his outline of "The Field of Sociology," chapter 1 of *The Sociology of Georg Simmel*, ed. and trans. Kurt H. Wolff (New York: The Free Press, 1950). The question of whether or not sociology can call itself a science is discussed in pp. 3–11. Further references to sociology as a science and by implication, Simmel's work as science appear on pp. 11, 13, 21, and 22.

9. Coser, *Simmel*, p. 3. I suspect that by virtue of Coser's admiration for Simmel's work, he does not wish for me to take this sentence as seriously as I do. Yet it does make intelligible many of Coser's statements on Simmel throughout the introduction and, as such, should be taken seriously.

10. Simmel has also earned himself the epithet "frivolous" as a result of his having chosen to analyze such oblique topics as "the prostitute" (Levine, *On Individuality*, pp. 121–26), "the stranger" (Wolff, *Sociology of Georg Simmel*, pp. 402–8), and "the handle of a vase" ("The Handle," trans. Rudolph H. Weingartner, in Kurt H. Wolff, ed., *Georg Simmel 1858–1918* [Columbus, Ohio: Ohio State University Press, 1959], pp. 267–75). Yet it is not the topic itself that brings on the change of frivolity. Certainly Simmel's "handle" is no more frivolous a topic than Freud's "dream." Freud, however, was not charged with frivolity. The charge is directed at Simmel because he chose to deal with the topic in a brief exposition; then he moved on to something else. Thus the charge of frivolity makes reference again to the fragmentary character of Simmel's writing and is similar to Coser's characterization of Simmel as "impatient" and "unable to concentrate."

11. Trans. Sara A. Solway and John H. Mueller (New York: The Free Press, 1938), pp. xxxvii–xxxviii.

12. See Alfred Schutz's discussion of commonsense knowledge in "Common-Sense and Scientific Interpretation of Human Action," in *Col-*

lected Papers I, ed. Maurice Natanson (The Hague: Martinus Nijhoff, 1971), pp. 3–47.

13. Durkheim, "Sociology and Its Scientific Field," p. 356.
14. Ibid., p. 355.
15. Ibid., p. 359.
16. See Alan Blum's chapter on Durkheim in *Theorizing* (London: Heinemann, 1974), pp. 185–217.
17. See Durkheim, "Sociology and Its Scientific Field," p. 354. See also Durkheim, *Suicide*, ed. George Simpson, trans. John A. Spaulding and George Simpson (New York: The Free Press, 1951), pp. 35–36.
18. We can see among the reactions to Simmel's work how members of the sociological community did their best to formalize his status as an outsider. For example, when they called his writing "artistic" or "philosophical" it was not for the purpose of truly evaluating its artistic and philosophical import; it meant that it was not sociology and that it need not be considered in relation to other sociological work. In "The Stranger" (Wolff, *Sociology of Georg Simmel*, p. 407) Simmel refers to this same phenomenon when he writes, "Strangers are not really conceived of as individuals, but as strangers of a particular type." Thus, for example, the popular concern for Simmel's "Jewish background" makes reference not simply to his slow advancement within the academic hierarchy, but also to the fact that members of the sociological community had trouble accounting for Simmel's uniqueness and individuality in any other way. It is not altogether curious that we seldom hear of Marx's and Durkheim's "Jewish background" when in fact they were "just as Jewish" as Simmel. Typing Simmel as a member of an alien group in our accounts of his work tends to make it less necessary to evaluate his uniqueness on its own ground. Thus in a very real sense, *we* make Simmel into an outsider.
19. Coser, *Simmel*, p. 55.
20. See Wolff, *Sociology of Georg Simmel*, chap. 2, pp. 26–39.
21. Ibid., p. 58.
22. Ibid., pp. 31–33.
23. Friedrich Nietzsche, *Thus Spoke Zarathustra*, in *The Portable Nietzsche*, trans. and ed. Walter Kaufmann (New York: The Viking Press, 1954), pp. 162–63.
24. Georg Simmel, "The Adventure," trans. David Kettler, in *Essays in Sociology, Philosophy and Aesthetics*, ed. Kurt H. Wolff (New York: Harper and Row, 1965), pp. 243–58.
25. Ibid., p. 244.
26. Ibid., p. 246.
27. Ibid., p. 248.
28. Consider the parallel that we may draw here between Simmel's notion

of "the adventure" and Kurt Wolff's notion of "surrender." Surrender refers to a mode of experience in the world. Like the adventure, surrender is determined by its separation from the structure, motive, and continuity of mundane life. Its characteristics, writes Wolff, are "total involvement" and "identification" with the immediate contents of experience, "suspension of received notions" with regard to these contents, "pertinence of everything" and "risk of being hurt" by the outcome of this experience. Surrender, as it is here conceived, constitutes a form of optimum participation. Here, little of preconceived structure and motive interferes with the experience to order the contents away from their direct relationship with the individual who experiences them. Like the adventure, the experience of surrender holds out the promise of wide intellectual growth in and through an experience of ecstasy. Says Wolff, such a unique relationship with contents can only be seen as one of "cognitive love." Thus the positive character of both the notions of "surrender" and "adventure" is determined by a unique experience of the fragment itself rather than by its relationship to what surrounds it. See Kurt H. Wolff, *Surrender and Catch* (Boston: D. Reidel Publishing Company, 1976), and "Surrender and Community Study: The Study of Loma," in Arthur J. Vidich, Joseph Bensman, and Maurice R. Stein, eds., *Reflections on Community Studies* (New York: John Wiley and Sons, 1964), pp. 233–63.

29. Simmel, "The Adventure," pp. 245 and 243, respectively.
30. Ibid., p. 245.
31. (New York: Basic Books, 1963), especially chaps. 1 and 2.
32. Wolff, *Sociology of Georg Simmel*, p. xix.
33. Ibid., p. xxxiii.
34. David Cooper writes "the whole point about dialectics is that one has to be the dialectics that one is about...." In "Beyond Words," in *The Dialectics of Liberation*, ed. David Cooper (Harmondsworth, England: Pelican, 1968), p. 193.
35. Coser, *Simmel*, pp. 10–14.
36. (Munich and Leipzig: Duncker and Humblot, 1918). Chapter 1 of this book has been translated into English and appears in Levine, *On Individuality*, pp. 353–374.
37. Coser, *Simmel*, p. 23.
38. See chapter 1 of *Lebensanschuung*, "The Transcendent Character of Life," in Levine, *On Individuality*, pp. 353–74.
39. Thomas Kuhn, *The Structure of Scientific Revolutions* (Chicago: University of Chicago Press, 1970), p. 149.
40. For a good example of the effect of Simmel's work on Weber, see Max Weber, "The Sociology of Charismatic Authority," in *From*

Max Weber, ed. and trans. H. H. Gerth and C. Wright Mills (New York: Oxford University Press, 1946), pp. 245–52.
41. In Levine, *On Individuality*, p. xiii.

Chapter 4

1. Maurice Friedman compiled a bibliography of approximately 520 items. He did not list separately articles which were collected in books edited by Buber. The bibliography appears in Paul Arthur Schillp and Maurice Friedman, eds., *The Philosophy of Martin Buber* (La Salle, Ill.: Open Court, 1967), pp. 747–86. See also a bibliography of 852 items compiled by Moshe Catanne, "A Bibliography of Martin Buber's Work (1895–1957)," (Jerusalem, Israel: Mosad Bialik, 1961).
2. Martin Buber, *I and Thou*, trans. Walter Kaufmann (New York: Charles Scribner's Sons, 1970).
3. In his forward to *Between Man and Man*, trans. Ronald Gregor Smith (London: Collins, 1961), Buber writes that the book arose out of a need to elaborate and apply what he had written in *I and Thou*. And in Aubrey Hodes, *Martin Buber: An Intimate Portrait* (New York: The Viking Press, 1971), the author often mentions Buber's personal concern for and preoccupation with the clarification and actualization of dialogue.
4. Schillp and Friedman, *Philosophy of Buber*.
5. Buber, "Replies to My Critics," in Schillp and Friedman, pp. 689–744.
6. Buber, "The Question to the Single One," in *Between Man and Man*, pp. 93–94. See also Buber, *I and Thou*, pp. 69–73.
7. Martin Buber, "Distance and Relation," trans. Ronald Gregor Smith, in *The Knowledge of Man*, ed. Maurice Friedman (New York: Harper Torchbooks, 1965), pp. 59–71.
8. A theme to be developed later in this paper and a theme that Buber emphasizes is the fact that a human being can put on an appearance of addressing another being when he is not really doing so. Thus I have distinguished here between "address" and "real address." For the remainder of the study I will drop the "real."
9. In *I and Thou*, Buber speaks about the possibility of participating in an authentic encounter with an inanimate being, pp. 57–59. See also Buber's "Afterword" to *I and Thou*, pp. 172–73.
10. Buber, "The Word That Is Spoken," trans. Maurice Friedman, in *The Knowledge of Man*, pp. 115–16.
11. In his article "Education" (1926), in *Between Man and Man*, p. 119,

Buber writes, "This fragile life between birth and death can nevertheless be a fulfillment—if it is a dialogue."

12. Buber, "Dialogue" (1929), in *Between Man and Man*, p. 37.

13. Ibid., p. 57.

14. Ibid., pp. 21–22.

15. Buber discusses elsewhere the theme of the broken-off conversation in *Eclipse of God*, trans. Maurice Friedman et al. (New York: Harper Torchbooks, 1957), pp. 11–18.

16. Buber, "Dialogue," p. 22.

17. Ibid., p. 20.

18. Buber, *I and Thou*, p. 69.

19. Buber, "The Word That Is Spoken," p. 112.

20. Buber, *I and Thou*, p. 69.

21. Ibid., p. 65.

22. Buber's notion of the realm of the "between" is discussed in "What Is Man?" in *Between Man and Man*, pp. 244–45.

23. Here "understanding" must be conceived of as an ontological category as well as an epistemological one. We should see "understanding" as a "standing under," or, as in the case of dialogue, a "standing within."

24. Elsewhere Buber speaks of the Hasidic notion of the highest man. He is "not the man who 'knows' the Torah, but the man who lives in it." "The Foundation Stone" (1943), in *The Origin and Meaning of Hasidism*, ed. and trans. Maurice Friedman (New York: Harper Torchbooks, 1966), p. 60.

25. Buber, "Replies to My Critics," p. 689.

26. Ibid., p. 697.

27. Buber, *I and Thou*, p. 82.

28. See Alfred Schutz, "Common-Sense and Scientific Interpretation of Human Action" in *Collected Papers I*, ed. Maurice Natanson (The Hague: Martinus Nijhoff, 1971), pp. 3–47. See also Harold Garfinkel, "Common sense knowledge of social structures: the documentary method of interpretation in lay and professional fact finding," in *Studies in Ethnomethodology* (Englewood Cliffs, N.J.: Prentice-Hall, Inc., 1967), pp. 76–103.

29. Buber, "My Way to Hasidism" (1918), in *Hasidism and Modern Man*, trans. and ed. Maurice Friedman (New York: Harper Torchbooks, 1966). And in his "Autobiographical Fragments," in Schillp and Friedman, pp. 13–14, Buber discusses briefly his attitudes as a student to both the lecture form and the seminar form.

30. This problem—lecturing as objective speech—comes up in the context of Buber's dialogue with Carl Rogers which took place at a Midwest conference on Martin Buber held at the University of Michigan, April 18, 1957. See the editor's footnote to "Dialogue Between Martin

Buber and Carl R. Rogers," appended to *The Knowledge of Man*, p. 184.

31. Buber, "What to Do about the Ten Commandments," in *On the Bible*, ed. Nahum N. Glatzer (New York: Schocken Books, 1968), pp. 118–21. See also Buber, "The Words on the Tablets," in *Moses* (New York: Harper Torchbooks, 1958), pp. 119–140.

32. See Buber, "The Man of Today and the Jewish Bible," in *On the Bible*, pp. 1–13. See also Buber, "Biblical Humanism," in *On the Bible*, pp. 211–16.

33. Buber, *I and Thou*, p. 78.

34. Ibid., p. 62.

35. Ibid., p. 58.

36. Buber, "Dialogue," p. 53.

37. When it is another person that is being controlled, this is no Other in any relevant sense, but merely a thing among things. Here Other (i.e., the potential Other) is transformed into a use object.

38. Buber, "Replies to My Critics," p. 704.

39. Buber, *I and Thou*, pp. 98–99.

40. To illustrate this same theme, Robert Wood, in *Martin Buber's Ontology* (Evanston: Northwestern University Press, 1969), p. 28, constructs a fitting poetic image. Of *I and Thou*, he writes that dialogue "hovers over the text." Here Wood also suggests that the essence of dialogue cannot be tied down and written into the literal text itself. But while the text cannot preserve dialogue concretely within its pages, it can present dialogue to the reader as an almost-visible possibility—an unfinished potential. The objective content of the book, while itself unfinished, still turns in the direction of its own fulfillment. And the image of dialogue hovering over the text is especially striking here and suggests that this potential, like an angel, will descend upon certain readers while fleeing from others. "Hovering" dialogue, suspended possibility for human speech, not yet tied to anyone, waits for its location in a particular situation for a particular duration. The responsibility lies with the reader.

41. Walker Percy, *The Message in the Bottle* (New York: Farrar, Strauss and Giroux, 1975), p. 285.

42. Thomas Kuhn, *The Structure of Scientific Revolutions* (Chicago: The University of Chicago Press, 1970), p. viii.

43. On the same theme, Buber recalls a story told of the Hasidic master, Rabbi Pinhas of Koretz. In his time, the prayer book of the famous Kabbalist, Isaac Luria, had been published and the students of Rabbi Pinhas had acquired a copy. They requested of their rabbi that he allow them to pray from this book expecting that the book would somehow enhance the quality of their prayers. Rabbi Pinhas permitted

them to do so, but to the students' regret, the book did not furnish the anticipated magic. In fact, the students felt that praying from Isaac Luria's prayer book seemed to have lowered the emotional content of their prayers. For this reason they came to complain to Rabbi Pinhas. Their rabbi only had to remind them of the source from which prayer arises. Prayer comes from the heart's waiting, he said. No formulae are required; if anything, a formula can only stand in the way. Isaac Luria's prayer book does not contain Isaac Luria's prayers. It owns nothing by way of authentic prayer that may be injected into a reader. Buber tells this story twice: in "Spirit and Body of the Hasidic Movement" (1921) in *The Origin and Meaning of Hasidism*, pp. 136–37, and in *Tales of the Hasidim: Early Masters* (New York: Schocken Books, 1947), p. 125.

44. Buber, "Replies to My Critics," p. 693.
45. Ibid., p. 693, when Buber writes, "I have no teaching," the sentence is followed by "I only point to something." Consider Heidegger's notion of the essential act of pointing in *What Is Called Thinking?* (1954), trans. Fred D. Wieck and J. Glenn Gray (New York: Harper and Row, 1968), p. 9. There the author writes, "What withdraws from us, draws us along by its very withdrawal, whether or not we become aware of it immediately, or at all. . . . As we are drawing toward what withdraws, we ourselves are pointers pointing toward it."
46. Alan Blum, "Positive Thinking," *Theory and Society*, vol. 1, no. 3, p. 246.
47. Buber, "Dialogue," p. 56.
48. Ibid., p. 59.
49. Wood, *Buber's Ontology*, p. 89.
50. Michael Theunissen, "Bubers negative Ontologie des Zwischen," *Philosophisches Jahrbuch* 71, no. 2 (1964).
51. Kuhn, *Scientific Revolutions*, p. 79.

Chapter 5

1. The image of "great criticism" lying in the drugstore is taken from Herbert Marcuse, *One-Dimensional Man* (Boston: Beacon Press, 1964), p. 64.
2. Ibid.

BIBLIOGRAPHY

Aristotle. *Metaphysics*. In *The Basic Works of Aristotle*. Edited by Richard McKeon. New York: Random House, 1941.

Blum, Alan F. "Positive Thinking." *Theory and Society* 1, no. 3.

————. *Theorizing*. London: Heinemann, 1974.

Breuer, Joseph, and Freud, Sigmund. *Studies in Hysteria* (1893–95). In Freud, *The Standard Edition of the Complete Psychological Works of Sigmund Freud*, 24 volumes. Translated under the General Editorship of James Strachey. London: Hogarth Press and the Institute of Psycho-Analysis, 1966. Volume 2.

Buber, Martin. "Autobiographical Fragments." In *The Philosophy of Martin Buber*. Edited by Paul Arthur Schillp and Maurice Friedman. La Salle, Ill.: Open Court, 1967.

————. *Between Man and Man*. Translated by Ronald Gregor Smith. London: Collins, 1961.

————. "Biblical Humanism." In *On the Bible*. Edited by Nahum N. Glatzer. New York: Schocken Books, 1968.

————. "Dialogue." In *Between Man and Man*. Translated by Ronald Gregor Smith. London: Collins, 1961.

————. "Dialogue between Martin Buber and Carl R. Rogers." In *The Knowledge of Man*. Edited by Maurice Friedman. New York: Harper Torchbooks, 1965.

————. "Distance and Relation." Translated by Ronald Gregor Smith. In *The Knowledge of Man*. Edited by Maurice Friedman. New York: Harper Torchbooks, 1965.

————. *Eclipse of God.* Translated by Maurice Friedman et al. New York: Harper Torchbooks, 1957.

————. "Education." In *Between Man and Man.* Translated by Ronald Gregor Smith. London: Collins, 1961.

————. *I and Thou.* Translated by Walter Kaufmann. New York: Charles Scribner's Sons, 1970.

————. *Moses.* New York: Harper Torchbooks, 1958.

————. "My Way to Hasidism." In *Hasidism and Modern Man.* Translated and edited by Maurice Friedman. New York: Harper Torchbooks, 1966.

————. "Replies to My Critics." In *The Philosophy of Martin Buber.* Edited by Paul Arthur Schillp and Maurice Friedman. La Salle, Ill.: Open Court, 1967.

————. "Spirit and Body of the Hasidic Movement." In *The Origin and Meaning of Hasidism.* Translated and edited by Maurice Friedman. New York: Harper Torchbooks, 1966.

————. *Tales of the Hasidim: Early Masters.* Translated by Olga Marx. New York: Schocken Books, 1947.

————. "The Foundation Stone." In *The Origin and Meaning of Hasidism.* Edited and translated by Maurice Friedman. New York: Harper Torchbooks, 1966.

————. "The Man of Today and the Jewish Bible." In *On the Bible.* Edited by Nahum N. Glatzer. New York: Schocken Books, 1968.

————. "The Question to the Single One." In *Between Man and Man.* Translated by Ronald Gregor Smith. London: Collins, 1961.

————. "The Word That Is Spoken." Translated by Maurice Friedman. In *The Knowledge of Man.* Edited by Maurice Friedman. New York: Harper Torchbooks, 1965.

————. "What Is Man?" In *Between Man and Man.* Translated by Ronald Gregor Smith. London: Collins, 1961.

————. "What to Do about the Ten Commandments." In *On the Bible.* Edited by Nahum N. Glatzer. New York: Schocken Books, 1968.

Catanne, Moshe. "A Bibliography of Martin Buber's Works (1895–1957)." Jerusalem, Israel: Mosad Bialik, 1961.

Cooper, David. "Beyond Words." In *The Dialectics of Liberation.* Edited by David Cooper. Harmondsworth, England: Pelican, 1968.

Coser, Lewis, ed. *Georg Simmel.* Englewood Cliffs, N.J.: Prentice-Hall, 1965.

Durkheim, Emile. "Sociology and Its Scientific Field." In *Emile Durkheim, 1858–1917.* Edited by Kurt H. Wolff. Columbus, Ohio: Ohio State University Press, 1960.

————. *Suicide.* Edited by George Simpson, translated by John A. Spaulding and George Simpson. New York: The Free Press, 1951.

———. *The Rules of Sociological Method*. Translated by Sara A. Solway and John H. Mueller. New York: The Free Press, 1938.

Ellenberger, Henri F. *The Discovery of the Unconscious*. New York: Basic Books, 1970.

Feuer, Lewis. *The Scientific Intellectual*. New York: Basic Books, 1963.

Feyerabend, Paul. "Consolations for the Specialist." In *Criticism and the Growth of Knowledge*. Edited by Imre Lakatos and Alan Musgrave. Cambridge: Cambridge University Press, 1970.

Freud, Sigmund. "A Case of Successful Treatment of Hypnotism" (1892–93). In *The Standard Edition of the Complete Psychological Works of Sigmund Freud* (hereafter cited as S.E.), 24 volumes. Translated under the General Editorship of James Strachey. London: Hogarth Press and the Institute of Psycho-Analysis, 1953–1974. Volume 1.

———. "A Religious Experience" (1928). S.E., vol. 21.

———. *An Autobiographical Study* (1925). S.E., vol. 20.

———. *Civilization and Its Discontents* (1930). S.E., vol. 21.

———. "Creative Writers and Day-Dreaming" (1908). S.E., vol. 9.

———. "Delusions and Dreams in Jensen's *Gradiva*" (1907). S.E., vol. 9.

———. "Formulations on the Two Principles of Mental Functioning" (1911). S.E., vol. 12.

———. "Fragment of an Analysis of a Case of Hysteria" (1905). S.E., vol. 7.

———. "From the History of an Infantile Neurosis" (1918). S.E., vol. 17.

———. *Group Psychology and the Analysis of the Ego* (1921). S.E., vol. 18.

———. *Introductory Lectures on Psycho-Analysis* (1916–17). S.E., vols. 15 and 16.

———. "Obsessive Actions and Religious Practices" (1907). S.E., vol. 9.

———. "On Beginning the Treatment: Further Recommendations on the Technique of Psycho-Analysis I" (1913). S.E., vol. 12.

———. *On the History of the Psycho-Analytic Movement* (1914). S.E., vol. 14.

———. "Preface to Reik's *Ritual: Psycho-Analytic Studies*" (1919). S.E., vol. 17.

———. "Psycho-Analysis and the Establishment of the Facts in Legal Proceedings" (1906). S.E., vol. 9.

———. "Repression" (1915). S.E., vol. 14.

———. "Screen Memories" (1899). S.E., vol. 3.

———. "The Aetiology of Hysteria" (1896). S.E., vol. 3.

———. *The Future of an Illusion* (1927). S.E., vol. 21.

———. *The Interpretation of Dreams* (1900). S.E., vols. 4 and 5.

———. "The Moses of Michelangelo" (1914). S.E., vol. 13.

———. *The Psychopathology of Everyday Life* (1901). S.E., vol. 6.

————. "The Taboo of Virginity" (1918). *S.E.*, vol. 11.

————. "The Theme of the Three Caskets" (1913). *S.E.*, vol. 12.

————. *Totem and Taboo* (1913). *S.E.*, vol. 13.

————. "Why War?" (1933). *S.E.*, vol. 22.

————. *The Origins of Psycho-Analysis: Letters to Wilhelm Fliess.* Edited by Ernst Kris, Marie Bonaparte and Anna Freud, translated by Eric Mosbacher and James Strachey. New York: Basic Books, 1954.

Freud, Sigmund, and Breuer, Joseph. *Studies in Hysteria* (1893–95). *S.E.*, vol. 2.

Garfinkel, Harold. *Studies in Ethnomethodology.* Englewood Cliffs, N.J.: Prentice-Hall, 1967.

Grassi, Ernesto. "Critical or Topical Philosophy? Meditations on the De nostri temperis studiorum ratione." Translated by Hayden V. White. In *Giambattista Vico, An International Symposium.* Edited by Giorgio Tagliacozzo. Baltimore: Johns Hopkins Press, 1969.

Heidegger, Martin. *An Introduction to Metaphysics.* Translated by Ralph Manheim. Garden City, N.Y.: Anchor Books, 1961.

————. *What Is Called Thinking?* Translated by Fred D. Wieck and J. Glenn Gray. New York: Harper and Row, 1968.

————. *What Is Philosophy?* Translated by Jean T. Wilde and William Kluback. New Haven, Conn.: College and University Press, 1956.

Hegel, Friedrich. *Hegel: Texts and Commentary.* Edited and translated by Walter Kaufmann. Garden City, N.Y.: Anchor Books, 1966.

Hodes, Aubrey. *Martin Buber: An Intimate Portrait.* New York: The Viking Press, 1971.

Jones, Ernest. *Sigmund Freud: Life and Work,* 3 volumes. London: Hogarth Press, 1953.

Kierkegaard, Søren. "The Sickness unto Death." In *Fear and Trembling and the Sickness unto Death.* Translated by Walter Lowrie. Princeton, N.J.: Princeton University Press, 1941.

Kris, E., Bonaparte, M., and Freud, A., eds. *The Origins of Psycho-Analysis: Letters to Wilhelm Fliess.* Translated by Eric Mosbacher and James Strachey. New York: Basic Books, 1954.

Kuhn, Thomas. "Reflections on My Critics." In *Criticism and the Growth of Knowledge.* Edited by Imre Lakatos and Alan Musgrave. Cambridge University Press, 1970.

————. *The Structure of Scientific Revolutions.* Chicago: University of Chicago Press, 1970.

Marcuse, Herbert. *One-Dimensional Man.* Boston: Beacon Press, 1964.

Nietzsche, Friedrich. *Thus Spoke Zarathustra.* In *The Portable Nietzsche.* Translated and edited by Walter Kaufmann. New York: Viking Press, 1954.

Park, Robert E. "Human Migration and the Marginal Man." In *Race and Culture*. New York. The Free Press, 1950.

Percy, Walker. *The Message in the Bottle*. New York: Farrar, Strauss and Giroux, 1975.

Plato. *Symposium*. Translated by Michael Joyce. In *The Collected Dialogues*. Edited by Edith Hamilton and Huntington Cairns. Princeton, N.J.: Princeton University Press, 1961.

Polanyi, Michael. *The Tacit Dimension*. Garden City, N.Y.: Anchor Books, 1966.

Popper, Karl. "Normal Science and Its Dangers." In *Criticism and the Growth of Knowledge*. Edited by Imre Lakatos and Alan Musgrave. Cambridge: Cambridge University Press, 1970.

Rank, Otto. *The Myth of the Birth of the Hero*. Edited by Phillip Freund, translated by F. Robbins and Smith Ely Jelliffe. New York: Vintage Books, 1932.

Ricoeur, Paul. *Freud and Philosophy*. Translated by Denis Savage. New Haven: Yale University Press, 1970.

Rosen, Stanley. "Σωφροσύνη and Selbstbewusstsein." In *Review of Metaphysics* 26, no. 4.

Schillp, Paul Arthur, and Friedman, Maurice, eds. *The Philosophy of Martin Buber*. La Salle, Ill.: Open Court, 1967.

Schutz, Alfred. "Common-Sense and Scientific Interpretation of Human Action." In *Collected Papers 1*. Edited by Maurice Natanson. The Hague: Martinus Nijhoff, 1971.

———. "The Stranger." In *Collected Papers II*. Edited by Arvid Brodersen. The Hague: Martinus Nijhoff, 1964.

Shroyer, Trent. "Toward a Critical Theory for Advanced Industrial Society." In *Recent Sociology No. 2*. Edited by Hans P. Dreitzel. New York: The Macmillan Company, 1970.

Simmel, Georg. *Lebensanchuung: Vier Metaphysische Kapitel*. Munich and Leipsig: Duncker and Humblot, 1918.

———. *On Individuality and Social Forms*. Edited by Donald N. Levine. Chicago: University of Chicago Press, 1971.

———. "The Adventure." Translated by David Kettler. In *Essays in Sociology, Philosophy and Aesthetics*. Edited by Kurt H. Wolff. New York: Harper and Row, 1965.

———. *The Sociology of Georg Simmel*. Edited and translated by Kurt H. Wolff. New York: The Free Press, 1950.

Sorokin, Pitirim. "A Critique of Simmel's Method." In *Georg Simmel*. Edited by Lewis Coser. Englewood Cliffs, N.J.: Prentice-Hall, 1965.

Stonequist, Everett. *The Marginal Man*. New York: Charles Scribner's Sons, 1937.

Theunissen, Michael. "Bubers negative Ontologie des Zwischen." In *Philosophisches Jahrbuch* 71, no. 2, 1964.

Veblen, Thorstein. "The Intellectual Pre-Eminence of Jews in Modern Europe." In *The Portable Veblen.* Edited by Max Lerner. New York: The Viking Press, 1948.

Vico, Giambattista. *The New Science of Giambattista Vico.* Revised translation by T. G. Bergin and M. H. Fisch. Ithaca: Cornell University Press, 1968.

von Wiese, Leopold. "Simmel's Formal Method." Translated by Martin Nicolaus. In *Georg Simmel.* Edited by Lewis Coser. Englewood Cliffs, N.J.: Prentice-Hall, 1965.

Weber, Max. *From Max Weber.* Edited and translated by H. H. Gerth and C. Wright Mills. New York: Oxford University Press, 1946.

Weingartner, Rudolf. *Experience and Culture: The Philosophy of Georg Simmel.* Middletown, Conn.: Wesleyan University Press, 1960.

Wittgenstein, Ludwig. *Philosophical Investigations.* Translated by G. E. M. Anscombe. Oxford: Basil Blackwell, 1968.

Wolff, Kurt H., ed. *Emile Durkheim, 1858–1917.* Columbus, Ohio: Ohio State University Press, 1960.

———. *Georg Simmel, 1858–1918.* Columbus, Ohio: Ohio State University Press, 1959.

———. *Surrender and Catch.* Boston: D. Reidel Publishing Company, 1976.

———. "Surrender and Community Study: The Study of Loma." In *Reflections on Community Studies.* Edited by Arthur J. Vidich, Joseph Bensman, and Maurice R. Stein. New York: John Wiley and Sons, 1964.

Wood, Robert E. *Martin Buber's Ontology.* Evanston: Northwestern University Press, 1969.

INDEX

Library of Congress Cataloging in Publication Data
Axelrod, Charles David.
Studies in intellectual breakthrough.
Bibliography: p.
Includes index.
1. Creative thinking. 2. Originality.
3. Freud, Sigmund, 1856–1939. 4. Simmel, Georg,
1858–1918. 5. Buber, Martin, 1878–1965. I. Title.
BF408.A93   153.3'5'0926 [B]   78-53177
ISBN 0–87023–256–8